BRITISH RAILWAY JOURNEYS

EUSTON TO THE MIDLANDS AND NORTHWEST

4

Caroline Dakers

Fourth Estate · London
in association with the
English Tourist Board

© Caroline Dakers 1986

First published in 1986
Fourth Estate Limited
113 Westbourne Grove, London W2 4UP

Design and maps by Richard Kelly
Text illustrations by Robert Shadbolt
Cover illustration by Michael O'Brien

British Library Cataloguing in Publication Data

Dakers, Caroline
British railway journeys.
4: Euston to the Midlands and Northwest
1. Great Britain—Description and travel—1971—
Guide-books
I. Title   II. English Tourist Board
914.1′04858   DA650

~~ISBN 0 947795 53 3~~

Typeset in Gill by
M.C. Typeset, Chatham, Kent.
Printed and bound by
Richard Clay (The Chaucer Press) Ltd,
Bungay, Suffolk.

Contents

Acknowledgements

I owe particular thanks to Robert Thorne, who first suggested the series and gave me much help and advice, and to the following members of the Victorian Society: Alan Crawford, John Minnie and Ian Wells. Other members of the Victorian Society gave me many useful snippets of information. I would like to thank especially W. A. Porter, the Regional Public Affairs Manager, BRER York; and also J. Dennis, Hugh Douglas, John Dawson, David Lawrence and G. J. Smith of British Rail and the many helpful station masters and ticket collectors; A. H. Hogden of the Environmental Services Swindon; Colin Woodley of Thorn EMI; R. A. Shaw, local history librarian at Battersea District Library; F. W. Manders at the Central Library Newcastle; Peter de Figueiredo, Chief Planning Officer of Macclesfield Borough Council; John Storrs of the Berol Company; Bernard Joy; Ian McCaig; Sir Peter Allen; Ron Cohen of the London Brick Company; Mr Tungay of DRG Envelopes; press officers at British Steel, the CEGB, Wander Foods (Ovaltine), Ford at Halewood, ICI; the Milton Keynes Development Corporation; the GLC Press Office; librarians at Winchester and Basingstoke Public Libraries; the Information Department of BR Southern Region; and Maggie Hallett of East Surrey Health Authority. Friends and relatives who have helped me include: Lawrence Burton, Neil Burton, Barry and Audrey Cross, John Cross, Hazel Dakers, John, Elizabeth, Mark and Paul Dakers, John Falding, Kerry Kennedy, Michael Mason, Sarah Morcom, Michael Oakley and Pam Worskett. For updating the journeys out of Euston I would like to thank Elizabeth Rosser.

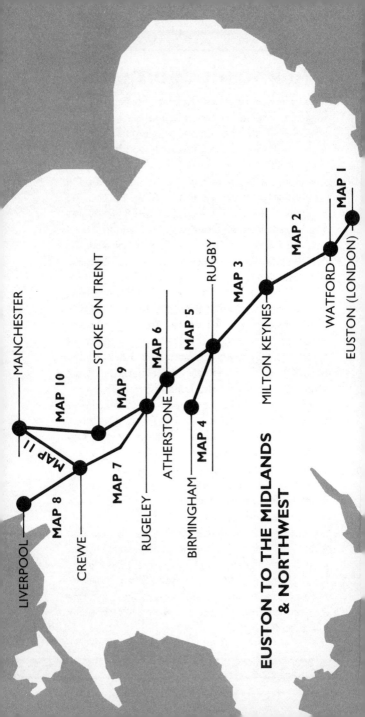

EUSTON TO THE MIDLANDS & NORTHWEST

MAP 1
MAP 2
MAP 3
MAP 4
MAP 5
MAP 6
MAP 7
MAP 8
MAP 9
MAP 10
MAP 11

EUSTON (LONDON)
WATFORD
MILTON KEYNES
RUGBY
ATHERSTONE
BIRMINGHAM
RUGELEY
STOKE ON TRENT
MANCHESTER
CREWE
LIVERPOOL

How to use this guide

Rather than adopt a continuous narrative which would only be of benefit to passengers travelling out of London, I have adopted a gazetteer approach. Landmarks appear in **bold type** for quick reference. All journeys have been compiled travelling from London – facing the engine – to the InterCity destination. A capital *L* signifies the landmark's position to the *left* of the track travelling away from London. A small *r* signifies the landmark's position to the *right* of the track travelling towards London. Thus: (*L:r*) **Regents Park** signifies that Regents Park is to the left of the track travelling away from London (Euston) and to the right travelling towards London. If travelling with your back to the engine then the letters must be reversed: Regents Park is to the right of the track leaving London and to the left approaching London.

Each major landmark is numbered and may be referred to on a map prefacing the journey or section of the journey.

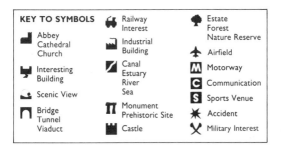

KEY TO SYMBOLS

- Abbey Cathedral Church
- Interesting Building
- Scenic View
- Bridge Tunnel Viaduct
- Railway Interest
- Industrial Building
- Canal Estuary River Sea
- Monument Prehistoric Site
- Castle
- Estate Forest Nature Reserve
- Airfield
- Motorway
- Communication
- Sports Venue
- Accident
- Military Interest

There are two routes to Manchester from Euston: half of InterCity trains travel via Stafford, Stoke on Trent and Macclesfield; half travel via Stafford, Crewe and Wilmslow. This book covers both routes.

EUSTON
TO
BIRMINGHAM

Introduction

The industrialists and businessmen of Birmingham put forward the idea of a railway line connecting their rapidly expanding Midland empires with the markets and port of London. Birmingham was increasing its wealth and population at a tremendous rate. In 1801 the population was 86,000; by 1831 it was 147,000. A variety of small industries were established – the largest was Boulton and Watt's Soho Manufactory. Nearby Coventry was also experiencing the effects of the Industrial Revolution and its textile industry – still based on home weaving – was expanding. However, the only forms of transport available were canal barge and coach. Twenty-six fast flyboats a day transported light and perishable goods on the Grand Junction Canal to London and there were 16 coaches a day carrying sheep and cattle (8,000 head a week) to London. But these methods were slow and uneconomic and Midland industries were faced with increasing competition from the continent.

The London and Birmingham Railway Bill passed through Parliament in May 1833 but not without a struggle. Canal and coach owners were not unnaturally afraid of the competition from the railway for, as was the case wherever a railway was built in Britain, they would inevitably be put out of business. Some of the landed gentry, through whose parks and estates Robert Stephenson proposed to run his line, were also far from happy about the intended line. Sir Astley Cooper of Hemel Hempstead went so far as to declare: 'if this sort of thing be permitted to go on, you will, in a very few years, destroy the *noblesse*'.

The result of the opposition was that the L&BR Co. had to pay £750,000 to buy off the interested parties. Just to get the Bill through Parliament cost the company £72,000. Some landowners were able to make a tidy sum out of the railway: 'A reverend gentleman complained that his privacy had been ruined, that his daughter's bedroom windows were exposed to the unhallowed gaze of the men working on the railway, and that he must remove his family to a watering-place, to enable him to do which he must engage a curate. All this was considered in the compensation demanded, and paid; yet no curate has been engaged, no lodgings at a watering-place taken. The unhappy family have still dwelt in their desecrated abode, and borne with Christian-like resignation all the miseries heaped upon them. The gilding of the pill, it seems, has rendered it palatable, and we have no doubt that if his daughter's rooms have a back window as well as a front one, he would be exceedingly glad if a railroad was carried across at the same price' (C. B. Andrews, *The Railway Age*, 1937).

Robert Stephenson was employed by the L&BR as engineer. He decided on a maximum gradient between Camden Town and Birmingham of no more than 1 in 330 which forced him to undertake some enormous earthworks. Nearly 20,000 navvies were employed to carry out works which one contemporary writer compared to the building of the Great Pyramid of Egypt. Peter Lecount calculated that the labour of the Great Pyramid was equivalent to lifting 15,733,000,000 cubic feet of stone one foot high. To build the railway 25,000,000,000 cubic feet of a similar weight of material had to be lifted one foot – 9,267,000,000 cubic feet more than for the Great Pyramid. Charles Dickens described the effect of such efforts in Camden Town in *Dombey and Son*: 'The first shock of a great earthquake had . . . rent the whole neighbourhood to its centre. Traces of its course were visible on every side. Houses were knocked down; streets broken through and stopped; deep pits and trenches dug in the ground; enormous heaps of earth and clay thrown up; buildings that were undermined and shaking propped by great beams of wood ... Everywhere were bridges that led nowhere; thoroughfares that were wholly impassable; Babel towers of chimneys wanting half their height; temporary wooden houses and enclosures in the most unlikely situations; carcases of ragged tenements, and fragments of unfinished walls and arches, and piles of scaffolding, and wildernesses of bricks, and giant forms of cranes, and tripods straddling above nothing. There were a hundred thousand shapes and substances of incompleteness wildly mingled out of their place, upside down, burrowing in the earth, aspiring in the air, mouldering in the water, and unintelligible as any dream ... the yet unfinished and unopened railroad ... from the very core of all this dire disorder trailed smoothly away upon its mighty course of civilisation and improvement.'

Thirty main contractors undertook to build sections of the line and ten of these failed completely. Jackson and Seeldon lasted only a few months on the contract for the Primrose Hill Tunnel (see p. 26). Stephenson had to take over the work which cost £286,000, over twice the original estimate.

T. Townsend worked for a year on the cutting north of Tring until giving in. One and a half million cubic yards of chalk had to be removed to create a cutting through the Chilterns ¼ mile long and up to 57 feet deep. The cutting between Roade and Blisworth took 800 men 3,000 barrels of gunpowder to remove 1 million cubic yards of spoil. Later over 100 iron girders had to be placed across the line to keep back the retaining walls, following slips along the cutting.

The Kilsby Tunnel (see p. 51) caused the greatest problems, bankrupting the contractor –

who then died – killing 26 men and holding up the completion of the line. It is 2,423 yards long and when completed was the largest railway tunnel in the world. Its position was soon overtaken by further engineering feats as a writer pointed out in 1851. '. . . once one of the wonders of the world; but . . . reduced to the level of any other long dark hole'. A hidden spring was discovered soon after work on the tunnel began and 13 pumping engines had to work for 19 months to pump out the water (1,800 gallons a minute). The navvies who built the tunnel had a reputation for strength and reckless-ness. Three were killed while competing at jumping over the mouth of one of the ventilation shafts. Stephenson was praised by an early railway histo-rian for giving his men the extra willpower to complete Kilsby: 'Stephenson infused into the workmen so much of his own energy that when either of their companions were killed by their side they merely threw the body out of sight and forgot his death in their own exertions.' When the tunnel was completed costs amounted to £291,030: the estimate had been for £98,988.

Stephenson confessed to a friend his unease about the work on the L&BR. With such heavy earthworks the cost per mile was far higher than many other lines: 'I sometimes feel very uneasy about my position. My courage at times almost fails me and I fear that some fine morning my reputation may break out under me like an eggshell.' Howev-er, one of his pupils, F. R. Conder, revealed the enormous power of the engineer: 'It is rare that a civilian has so free and almost martial an address, it is still more rare for such features to be seen in any man who has inherited them from a line of gently nurtured ancestors . . . He knew how to attach people to him; he also knew how to be a firm and persistent hater.'

The first section of the line to be completed was

from Euston to Boxmoor (for Hemel Hempstead) and it was opened on 20 June 1837. The sections from Boxmoor to Denbigh Hall (just north of Bletchley) and from Birmingham to Rugby were opened on 9 April 1838. Passengers had to travel by coach between Denbigh Hall and Rugby until the earthworks in between were completed and the line was eventually opened on 17 September 1838. The break in the line caused irritation and delay and some people were unable to fit on the coaches. Bletchley was said to be (c. 1838) 'a small miserable village, where those disappointed in getting on from Denbigh Hall must not expect to find accommodation even for their dog'.

The service opened with six trains each way. The fastest journey time was 5 hours 37 minutes. The 1st class fare to Rugby was 24s 6d one way; 2nd class, 15s. This was not particularly cheap and 2nd class passengers had to travel in coaches 'open at the side, without linings, cushions or divisions in the compartments', but large numbers still flocked to use the railway. Osborne, in his L&BR Guide of 1838, commented on the immediate social effects: 'It has already begun to produce great and material changes in society. Many who, but a few years since, scarcely penetrated beyond the county in which they were born are now induced to visit places far more remote . . . and become acquainted with customs, manners and habits which previously were unknown to them.'

The traffic in goods and livestock was equally heavy. For the Christmas cattle market in London in 1843 the L&BR carried, in two days, 1,085 oxen, 1,420 sheep and 93 pigs in 263 wagons. In 1859 the up line between Primrose Hill and Bletchley was duplicated, in 1874 a new tunnel at Watford was opened and by 1882 the whole of the line had been quadrupled.

A new town was established at Wolverton

around the locomotive and carriage workshops of the L&BR. Wolverton is halfway between London and Birmingham and in 1831 was a small hamlet with a population of 417. Seven years later the locomotive works opened with a workforce of 400. Houses were built by the railway company together with a church, schools and supplies of gas and water. From 1854 housing developed to the east of Wolverton, at Bradwell, as the original landowner refused to sell any more of his land to the company. The peak of the works was from 1886 to 1900 when 5,000 men were employed and the workshops covered 35 acres. In 1851 Samuel Sidney commented in his *Rides on Railways* on the workforce he found at Wolverton, their conditions and opportunities: 'we have here a body of mechanics of intelligence above average regularly employed for 10½ hours, during five days, and for eight hours during the sixth day of the week, well paid, well housed, with schools for their children, a reading-room and mechanics' institution at their disposal, gardens for their leisure hours, and a church and clergyman exclusively devoted to them. When work is ended, Wolverton is a pure republic – equality reigns.'

At the London end the goods station at Camden Town was developed with facilities for building and repairing wagons and trucks. In the 1850s the yard had enough passenger carriages to give 11 miles of seat room or to seat 40,196 individuals. There were arrangements for building wagons and trucks, conveying coals and other merchandise and livestock. A newspaper reporter in the 1860s described the scene: 'in the grey mists of the morning, in an atmosphere of a hundred conflicting smells, and by the light of faintly burning gas, we see a large portion of the supply of the great London markets rapidly disgorged by these night trains: fish, flesh and food, Aylesbury butter and dairy-fed pork, apples, cabbages and cucumbers.' The Roundhouse remains the last surviving memorial to the depot.

The L&BR merged with the Manchester and Birmingham Railway and the Grand Junction Railway (which had absorbed the Liverpool and Manchester Railway) to form the LNWR in July 1846. The great steam engines which ran on the LNWR were designed and built at the Crewe workshops which originally belonged to the Grand Junction Railway. David Joy created the 'Jenny Lind' class and John Ramsbottom the 'Lady of the Lake' class.

Steam running ended in 1968 on British Rail. The lines from Euston to Birmingham, Manchester and Liverpool had been electrified two years before: by 1974 electrification was extended as far as Glasgow, creating the longest stretch of electrified line in Britain. The trials of the Advanced Passenger Train took place on the line between Glasgow and Euston. Designed and built at Derby, the APT was the latest development in electric rail transport, aerodynamically shaped to reduce wind resistance and aid stability. The APT, however, has not been the success BR hoped and is off the tracks for the foreseeable future. Nevertheless, some of its new technological and design features are being incorporated in BR's rolling stock.

A newspaper article in 1982 revealed that the track between Euston and Birmingham was so worn out that on 25 occasions trains had to reduce their speeds from 100/75 mph down to 20/5 mph with the result that trains averaged 10 minutes late. The signalling system was apparently also worn out; there had been derailments, a serious land-slip, and structural faults in the Primrose Tunnel – yet more headaches for an already over-burdened British Rail. But since then there have been extensive engineering works on the line, for example improvements to the approaches to Birmingham

New Street. For the better-off passenger there is the opportunity to travel to Liverpool and Manchester in luxury Pullman carriages. However, all passengers will benefit from the new coaches and the locomotives now being built by BR for their InterCity services.

MAP I

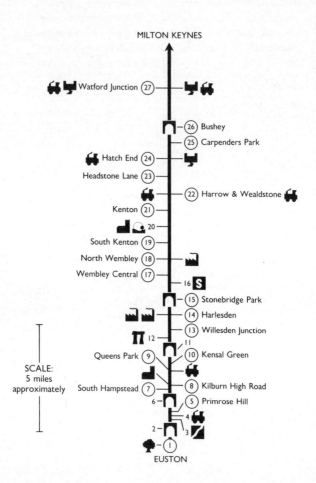

1 **EUSTON STATION** was London's first main line terminus, planned by Robert Stephenson and designed by Philip Hardwick. Its two great features were the Doric Triumphal Arch or Propylaeum, 72 feet high and built of Bramley Fall stone, and the Great Hall by Philip Charles Hardwick. Both were destroyed amid a storm of protest in 1961. Little remains of the Victorian station. The small entrance lodges faced with Portland stone which stand on either side of the approach used by buses from Euston Road were designed by J. B. Stansby as part of improvements to the station in 1869–74. Gilded letters on the quoin stones proclaim the names of the principal stations of the LNWR. The statue of Robert Stephenson by Baron Carlo Marochetti, presented to the LNWR by the Institute of Civil Engineers, now stands in the piazza of the station, dwarfed by the office blocks towering above it.

Objections to the Doric Propylaeum were made when it was first erected in 1838. Augustus Welby Pugin commented 'this piece of Brobdingnagian absurdity must have cost the Company a sum which would have built a first rate station.' The Arch, together with attendant lodges and 300-ft screen cost £35,000 but the Directors of the L&BR considered the money well spent. 'It may be said that the Railway is a great national undertaking, and that the national character is, in some respects, involved in the execution of the whole. All spectators are impressed by magnitude or mass, or by highly enriched detail in public buildings; and it is often remarked by critics that the English are too parsimonious and calculating to produce either the one or the other.' Parsimony ruled, however, when it came to rebuilding Euston. Though the LCC insisted the portico should be re-erected, the

Minister of Transport, Ernest Marples, announced its preservation did not justify the expenditure it would involve. The Ministry produced questionable figures of £12,000 for the demolition of the Propylaeum and £190,000 to move and rebuild it. Ernest Marples and the Prime Minister, Harold Macmillan, were unmoved by protests and demolition began on 6 November 1961. With the new terminus completed it is obvious that the portico could have been sited along Euston Road. It would have provided welcome relief to the coldly efficient, functional and characterless terminus behind.

Euston had two hotels, opened in September 1839 and designed by Philip Hardwick. The Victoria was for 2nd and 3rd class passengers, a 'dormitory and coffee room'; the Euston was for 1st class passengers. These were linked in 1881 by a new block, designed by J. Maclaren, which completely destroyed the view of Hardwick's screen from the Euston Road. Further expansion of the station in the 1880s involved disturbing the dead of St James's churchyard immediately west of the station. Considerably more care was taken over the removal of the bodies because of the criticism which had accompanied the loose treatment of corpses at St Pancras. Each corpse was given a new coffin and taken to St Pancras Cemetery in Finchley. 'A doctor and an inspector were constantly present at either end on behalf of the company, to see that nothing was done which might offend against either due reverence for the dead or due regard for the health of the living.'

Plans for the complete rebuilding of Euston began c.1900 but lack of money and the First World War delayed any decision. In 1935 the Railways (Agreement) Act granted a government loan towards the rebuilding of the station, hotels and offices; and Percy Thomas, President of the RIBA, produced an ambitious design. The Great Hall would be demolished, the portico would be re-erected on the Euston Road and a vast new terminus would be built with accommodation on the roof for helicopters. Sir Josiah Stamp, Chairman of the LMSR, even threw a switch to set off charges at the Caldon Low Quarries and release 100,000 tons of limestone for the rebuilding. War again intervened.

Neither war nor protests stopped the redevelopment plans of c.1960. The new terminus was designed by R. L. Moorcroft, architect of the London Midland Region, and opened by the Queen on 14 October 1968. Passengers pass through a 647-ft long colonnade of polished black granite and white mosaic horizontal facings which separates the piazza from the concourse. The concourse is 200 by 150 ft, clean, light, air conditioned, with a Travel Centre to the west, shops and lavatories to the east and ticket barriers to the north. From this characterless if airy and functional hall the passenger descends the sloping ramps to the gloomy platforms.

Leaving Euston Station For the first seven years (1837–44) the L&BR was open, trains were hauled by cable from Euston Station up to Camden Town. The power for the cables was supplied by two 60hp Maudslay and Field condensing engines which were below two large chimneys on either side of the line at Camden Town. Trains travelling towards Euston descended the bank from Camden unaided, after their engines were detached. The train still ascends the bank to Camden – though

without the cable – passing to the east of **Regents** *L:r.*
Park and through a cutting lined with black brick
walls. The high walls were built to keep back the
treacherous blue London clay but in the early years
of the railway they kept giving way under pressure.
Inverts were then built from wall to wall under the
railroad bed.

Approaching Euston (or leaving – back to the
engine) it is possible to see the **Post Office** *L:r.*
Tower, 620 feet high and now part of British
Telecom's empire.

2 **PARK STREET TUNNEL**   The Park Street
Tunnel is 161 yards long. Before the railway was
built this was an area of market gardens. There was
also a small colony of firework-makers whose
leader, called Bunyan, led an ineffectual resistance
to the railway: 'you who clamber over folkses walls
with your ladders and your hammer, your levels
and your bevels and your devils'.

3 **REGENTS CANAL**   The train crosses over the
Regents Canal with the imaginative **Pirate Castle**, *R:l*
a haven for children keen to learn canoeing and
sailing. The Regents Canal is the first part of the
Grand Union Canal system which can be seen on
the journey to the Midlands. It was built as an
extension from Paddington to the Thames at
Limehouse and opened on 1 August 1820.

4 **CAMDEN GOODS STATION AND THE
ROUNDHOUSE**   Robert Stephenson sug-
gested the L&BR should buy 30 acres of land in
Camden Town to develop as a goods station. 'At
Camden we may see sheep from Perth, vegetables
from Covent Garden for Glasgow, fish for Birming-

ham. Coal in immense quantities is brought from the Midland Counties, Worcs and Lancashire. Underground are stables and warehouses of the most extensive character; and the gas consumed annually at the station exceeds 6 million cubic feet' (George Measom, 1859). The two tall chimneys above the engines which cable-hauled the trains from Euston were on either side of the line; there were 2,500 feet of double track for goods waggons and 12 miles of single track. In 1850, 500 to 2,000 cattle and 2,000 to 6,000 sheep arrived weekly at the station but now the area is a deserted wasteland with only the Roundhouse surviving.

The Roundhouse was built in 1847 as a *R:1* repair shed and designed by Robert Stephenson, Dockray and Normanville. It covers 2,234 square yards and has a diameter of 160 feet. The iron roof is supported by 24 cast-iron columns and beneath the central turntable is a honeycomb of tunnels which gave access to the inspection pits and allowed for the removal of clinker. In 1964 the Roundhouse was presented to Centre 42, the arts

The Roundhouse

centre founded by Arnold Wesker to bring together the trade union movement and the arts; and in 1986 it became an arts centre for the black community.

5 **PRIMROSE HILL** (BR) Primrose Hill was first *R:1* called Greenbury Hill after the names of the three men executed for the murder of Sir Edmundsbury Godfrey. They carried his body to the hill (which is to the west of the line) after killing him near Somerset House. The station is on the North London line.

6 **PRIMROSE HILL TUNNEL** The Primrose Hill Tunnel is 1,182 yards long and has a handsome southern entrance flanked by Italianate towers on rusticated stone foundations. The materials beneath the black grime are cream stone and yellow stock brick, but even in their filthy state the portals are impressive. Stephenson and his secretary Budden were the designers. The contractors faced enormous problems in the digging of the tunnel and had to give up (see p.14). Stephenson assumed the tunnel could be built without an invert but the pressure of the clay was so great that the thickness of the brickwork had to be increased, an invert constructed and Roman cement used for the jointing instead of mortar.

7 **SOUTH HAMPSTEAD** (BR)

8 **KILBURN HIGH ROAD** (BR) The Victorian red-brick station buildings are difficult to see as they are on the bridge across the line. But there is a bright **mural** on the station wall. Kilburn was only *R:1* a small hamlet on Watling Street when the railway

was built: 'a place of residence by many genteel families . . . with a number of country villas.' It even had its own spa called Kilburn Wells. A traveller leaving London by train in 1838 declared on reaching Kilburn that he was 'freed from the accumulated bricks and mortar of the metropolis' and began 'to breathe a fresher air'. Dick Turpin began his famous ride to York on the gallant Bess at Kilburn. The spire visible between the blocks of flats belongs to **St Augustine's Church**, designed *L:r* by John Loughborough Pearson in 1871–98. The spire is in a Normandy-Gothic style and rises to 254 feet. Nikolaus Pevsner describes the church as 'one of the best churches of its date in the whole of England, a proud, honest, upright achievement'. Inside is an *Annunciation* by Titian and a *Virgin and Child* by Filippino Lippi.

9 **QUEENS PARK** (BR) The large four- *R:l* platformed station is bypassed by the main line trains but has a particularly elegant train shed. Queens Park was laid out in about 1900 as an experiment in better quality working-class housing. The station is also served by the Bakerloo underground line.

10 **KENSAL GREEN** (BR) *R:l*

11 **KENSAL GREEN TUNNEL** is 320 yards long and takes the train under the A404 to emerge next to Kensal Green Cemetery.

12 **KENSAL GREEN CEMETERY** The train is *L:r* below the cemetery in a cutting but there are glimpses of the tops of statues and gravestones. Kensal Green Cemetery was opened in 1832, the

first of the cemeteries which were built on a commercial scale and with new standards of mortuary hygiene. By the 1830s the graveyards of Inner London were in a ghastly state with drunken gravediggers replacing half-decomposed corpses with the bodies of the newly dead. A contemporary wrote with relief of the restoration of 'the good early Christian and even Pagan custom of interring the dead apart from the living'. The dead at Kensal Green include Brunel and his parents and the novelists Thackeray, Wilkie Collins and Trollope; also James Miranda Barry, Inspector General of the Army Medical Department who was discovered, on his death in 1865, to be a woman.

13 **WILLESDEN JUNCTION** (BR)   Little can be *R:l* seen of this important railway junction as the main line trains bypass the station to the south. It began as a small roadside station, opened in 1841–2 as Acton Lane. This was replaced in 1866 by Willesden Junction which consisted of two groups of completely separate high-level platforms. There was no indication from which platform the next train would be leaving so the Junction was nicknamed 'Bewildering Junction' and 'The Wilderness'. Rebuilding took place in 1894 and the Junction became an important distribution point for parcels and goods, with marshalling yards, a freight locomotive depot and north carriage depot. The station forms the background to *Waiting for the Train*, a painting by James (Jacques-Joseph) Tissot (1836–1902) which depicts his mistress-model waiting on the platform surrounded by luggage.

14 **HARLESDEN** (BR)   is distinguished by the *R:l* embattled **McVities factory** – 'McVities bake a *L:r*

better biscuit' – and the enormous red-brick **Heinz (57 Varieties) factory**.   *L:r*

15 STONEBRIDGE PARK (BR) In 1875 Stonebridge Park was no more than a 'cluster of 60 or 80 smart new villas for city men' but suburban development soon changed this. In 1953 carriage servicing was transferred from the Willesden depot to a large new installation at Stonebridge Park which gave local employment . a boost and thousands of new homes were built in the 1970s when the Stonebridge Comprehensive Development Area was formed.

Immediately north of Stonebridge Park is the **Brent Embankment and Viaduct**. The Embankment used up 372,000 cubic yards of earth which were brought from the cutting at Oxhey further up the line. The Viaduct once took the railway line over the River Brent; now it crosses over the A406 – the North Circular Road. It is built of stock bricks and was designed by Robert Stephenson.

16 WEMBLEY STADIUM Wembley Park was *R:l* first developed in the 1870s as a leisure centre and

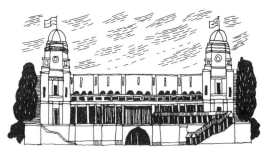

Wembley Stadium

there were ambitious plans to build an English Eiffel Tower before it was discovered the land could not support the weight. In 1924 the British Empire Exhibition was held at Wembley and the stadium, designed by Sir John Simpson and Maxwell Ayrton, was built to hold 100,000. The stadium, track facilities and swimming pool were used for the 1948 Olympic Games: more recently the stadium has been the venue for the FA and Rugby League Finals, for hockey, greyhound and speedway racing, and for Bob Geldof's 'Live Aid' concert in July 1985.

17 **WEMBLEY CENTRAL** (BR) In the 1840s the neighbourhood of Wembley was 'celebrated for stag hunting, on which occasions it is sometimes honoured by the presence of Her Majesty'. After the electrification of the railway line in 1920 the area changed dramatically with extensive residential and industrial building: the grounds of the 1924 British Empire Exhibition were intensively developed for the use of light industry.

18 **NORTH WEMBLEY** (BR) Semi-detached housing of the 1930s and a variety of factories, including **British Oxygen**, surround the red-brick *R:l* station.

19 **SOUTH KENTON** (BR)

20 **HARROW ON THE HILL** There is a good *L:r* view of Harrow on the Hill beyond the industrial estates which surround the railway line. **St Mary's Church spire** rises above the hill. The church is a *L:r* mixture of periods, dating from Norman times through to the 15th century. Inside is a memorial

by John Flaxman to John Lyon, farmer of the parish, who founded Harrow School. In the churchyard is an unusual tombstone to Thomas Port, engine driver, who was killed in 1838, the year the L&BR opened: 'Bright rose the morn and vig'rous rose poor Port/Gay on the train he used his wonted sport.' Harrow School began to expand in about 1800 and by the 1860s had become one of the most famous of the Victorian public schools. Trollope attended as a despised day pupil. Byron was also one of its pupils and wrote an early not very good poem 'On the distant view of the village and school':

Again I revisit the hills where we sported,
The streams where we swam, and the fields where
   we fought;
The school where, loud warn'd by the bell, we
   resorted,
To pore o'er the precepts by pedagogues taught.

The name Harrow is derived from *hergae*, the Saxon word for temple or shrine. Once, the hill was thickly wooded and popular with royal hunters. The present King's Head public house is on the site of Henry VIII's hunting lodge.

21 **KENTON** (BR)   *L:r*

22 **HARROW AND WEALDSTONE** (BR)
When the main line between Euston and Watford was widened for electrification in 1914–22 Gerard Horsley, a pupil of Norman Shaw, designed new stations. **Harrow and Wealdstone** is a Neo- *R:l*
Wren style building with a tower built of dark red brick with contrasting white terracotta string

courses. On the other side of the line are the older **yellow-brick platform buildings**. *L:r*

23 **HEADSTONE LANE** (BR) The red-brick sta- *L:r* tion is bypassed at high speed.

24 **HATCH END** (BR) The imposing red-brick Victorian building just before the station adorned with 'Franco-Flemish' gables and dormers was opened in 1853 as the **Commercial Travellers School**. It was designed by Lane and Ordish; wings *R:l* were added in 1868 by Knightley; a chapel was added in 1904 by H. D. Creswell. The Commercial Travellers Benevolent Institution was founded to clothe, maintain and educate destitute orphans of deceased commercial travellers and the children of 'necessitous travellers'.

   Hatch End Station is another of Gerard *L:r* Horsley's Neo-Wren stations (see Harrow and Wealdstone) in red brick and white stone and with two Queen Anne gables on the platform side, a cupola, clock and weathervane.

The train crosses the border between **Greater London** (formerly Middlesex) and **Hertford-shire**.

25 **CARPENDERS PARK** (BR) Carpenders Park Station was rebuilt in 1952 for the extensive new housing – both council and speculative – in the area. The style of the station building is distinctly functional and severe, reflecting the character of the nearby LCC housing estate. The station first opened in 1914 but was no more than a wooden halt serving the local golf course.

26 BUSHEY (BR)   Immediately north of Bushey the line crosses the **River Colne** over the **Colne Viaduct**. The viaduct was once one of the main sights in the area with its five semi-circular brick arches, 30 feet high and with parapet walls 312 feet long. It cost the L&BR £10,000 and now passes through the industrial wasteland which has occupied the land between Bushey and Watford.

27 WATFORD JUNCTION (BR)   Before the railway arrived at Watford the town was declining. Silk-spinning had stagnated, tanning and candle-making were dying out. Even so there were objections from property owners to the railway coming any closer than half a mile from the town centre. However, the decline was reversed and now Watford is a large flourishing town with a population of over 77,000. The concrete high-rise block towering above the town belongs to the **YMCA** and is a particularly ugly result of the *L:r* expansion. Immediately east of the station is the **Department of Employment**, aptly housed in *R:l* the **London Orphan Asylum**. The Gothic style buildings were designed by H. Dawson in 1869–71 and are built in yellow stock brick with a clock tower.

 Watford Junction Station   has a mixture of buildings: single-storey yellow-brick **platform** *R:l* **buildings**, older **red-brick buildings** with white- *L:r* painted awnings and decorative valancing. The railway deliberately encouraged the expansion of Watford by offering free 21-year season tickets to purchasers of houses above a certain price. The ticket remained with the property. The Bakerloo and Metropolitan Underground lines arrived in 1917 and 1925.

MAP 2

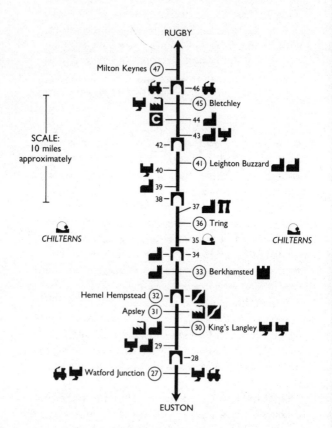

RUGBY

Milton Keynes (47)

— 46

(45) Bletchley

— 44

— 43

42 —

(41) Leighton Buzzard

40 —

39 —

38 —

— 37

(36) Tring

— 35

— 34

(33) Berkhamsted

Hemel Hempstead (32)

Apsley (31)

(30) King's Langley

29 —

— 28

Watford Junction (27)

EUSTON

SCALE:
10 miles
approximately

CHILTERNS

CHILTERNS

28 **WATFORD TUNNEL** The Earl of Essex and the Earl of Clarendon owned large estates at Watford – Cassiobury Park and The Grove – and Robert Stephenson was forced to build a tunnel 1 mile 57 yards long in order to get permission to cross their lands. Samuel Smiles commented 'this latter diversion ... inflicted on the public the inconvenience of the Watford tunnel ... and on the Company a largely increased outlay for its construction'. The Earls had been equally difficult when the Grand Junction Canal was being built across their land in 1794 and were able to obtain specially ornamental stretches of the canal for their parks as well as financial compensation. Stephenson and Budden gave the tunnel classical portals with semicircular arches 25 feet high and 24 feet wide surmounted by pediments. The tunnel was difficult to cut through the chalk and loose gravel, and ten men were buried under falling earth during the sinking of one of the shafts. 'One poor fellow was found, three weeks afterwards, standing perfectly upright with his trowel in his hand ... as employed at the moment of the dreadful occurrence' (Osborne's *London & Birmingham Railway Guide*, 1840).

29 **LANGLEYBURY CHURCH AND HOUSE** *L:r*
The flint church of **St Paul's** (with a west tower and spire) was designed by H. Woodyer and built in 1865. Behind, in the trees, is the early Georgian **Langleybury House**.

30 **KING'S LANGLEY** (BR) Just south of the station is the **Booksellers' Provident Retreat**, *R:l* immediately next to the railway line. This was built by the firm of John Dickinson who established

several paper mills in the valley at the beginning of the 19th century (see p. 37).

King's Langley was named after the Royal Palace which was on the hill to the west behind the **parish church** (with its embattled tower). *L:r* Edmund Langley, the fifth son of Edward III, was born at the Palace and lived there most of his life. He was buried at the adjacent Dominican Friary until the Dissolution of the Monasteries, when his body was transferred to the parish church. Piers Gaveston, the unfortunate favourite of Edward II was also buried in the Friary.

Ovaltine Factory

The large **factory** designed by Bowden and *L:r* Partners was begun in 1913 when **Ovaltine** (now Wander Foods) moved to King's Langley. Ovaltine was first manufactured in Switzerland: 1985 was the 75th anniversary of the first sales in Britain. In the late 1920s two farms were bought and the **thatched buildings and poultry farm** visible *R:l* from the train were built. In the 1930s Radio Luxembourg brought the bedtime drink into every home with its advertising jingle, 'We are the Ovaltinies, happy girls and boys'.

31 APSLEY (BR)   The paper manufacturing empire of John Dickinson has dominated the valley of the

River Gade from Watford to Hemel Hempstead since the beginning of the 19th century. With the financial help of his partner George Longman, Dickinson bought **Apsley Mill** in 1809 (close to *R:1* the station) and **Nash Mill** in 1811 (half a mile to *R:1* the south). The mills were very old – both named in Domesday Book as corn mills – and were converted to paper mills at the end of the 18th century. They are now owned by the Dickinson Robinson Group. Apsley is the biggest manufacturer of envelopes in Europe and Nash produces superior board for the printing industry.

The **Grand Union Canal** is now one of the *R:1* features of the journey between London and the Midlands. 'The way it seems to flirt with the railway line' (Alan Crawford), offering glimpses of bridges, locks and slow-moving narrow boats, is one of the most attractive parts of the journey. It can be followed almost all the way from Watford to Rugby. Water from the canal is still used to cool the turbines for the Dickinson mills: further supplies of water come from artesian wells sunk below the mills early in the 19th century.

32 HEMEL HEMPSTEAD (BR) Hemel Hempstead is to the north. The area immediately next to the station is **Boxmoor**, famous for its watercress beds growing along the **River Bulbourne**. Bob *R:1* Snooks came to an untimely end in 1802 close to the railway line. He was hanged from a chestnut tree for robbing the mail and was buried immediately beneath it.

The railway line crosses over the River Bulbourne and the Grand Union Canal just west of the station. When the canal was dug at Boxmoor there was a local outcry as it was planned to cross Boxmoor Commonland preserved for the benefit of the local people. The Company had to pay £900 for 25 acres of land and the money was used to build a new wharf on the canal and a workhouse.

33 BERKHAMSTED (BR)   There is a fine view of **Berkhamsted Castle** east of the line. The castle *R:l* was probably first erected in the late 11th century and in 1216 it was besieged by King Louis of France. Later it became an appendage of the Dukes of Cornwall and Chaucer lived there for a time when he was employed as clerk of the king's works and supervised the restoration of the buildings on the site. The main gateway and barbican were demolished by the L&BR to make way for the station. A mock Elizabethan structure was erected as compensation after the enraged inhabitants of Berkhamsted held a protest meeting in 1833, and was replaced when the line was widened in 1875. **St Peter's** is the large flint parish church.   *L:r*

34 NORTHCHURCH TUNNEL   The tunnel is 342 yards long and has handsome stone portals. The tower of **St Mary's Northchurch** can be *L:r* seen just north of the tunnel. There is a gravestone in the churchyard to Peter the Wild Boy who died in 1785. He was found in the Forest of Hartswold near Hanover in 1725 and thought to be about 12 years old. Nothing could be discovered of his background and how he came to be living in the forest. He was brought to England where 'proving incapable of speaking or of receiving any instruction, a comfortable provision was made for him by Her Majesty at a farm house in this parish, where he continued to the end of his inoffensive life'.

35 Between Berkhamsted and Tring the railway line passes through the beautiful **CHILTERN HILLS**. *R:I* To the north-east the land on the high ground belonged to the ancient estate of **Ashridge**, much of which is now owned by the National Trust. Originally there was a monastery at Ashridge. This became a royal residence at the Dissolution of the Monasteries and then passed to the Dukes of Bridgewater and Earls Brownlow. In 1929 the mansion became the Bonar Law Memorial College for Unionist Workers; now it is a Management College.

36 TRING (BR)   Tring is about two miles away to the west. The townsfolk were so keen for the railway to come to their town that they built the road to the station. The station was first of all to be some 3½ miles away at the north end of Tring Cutting because the L&BR refused to pay the high price demanded by the profiteering landowner. The townsfolk intervened and paid the difference between the railway company's offer and the demand of the greedy landowner.

37 ALDBURY CHURCH   The tower of Aldbury *R:I* Church can just be seen about a mile from the station and beyond it, on top of the ridge, a **monument** to the 3rd Duke of Bridgewater. The *R:I* Greek Doric column has an urn on top and was erected in 1832 to commemorate the Duke's work for the promotion of canals (see p. 119).

38 TRING CUTTING   Samuel Smiles described the cutting as an 'immense chasm across the great chalk ridge'. 1½ million cubic yards of chalk were removed and some used to make the following

6-mile long embankment. The problems involved in cutting through the chalk and gravel defeated the contractor (see p. 14). When the railway navvies made the cutting they found the tusk and teeth of an elephant. At the point where the line crosses the **Icknield Way** at the northenmost end they unearthed Roman pottery and 16 human skeletons. The Icknield Way was the highway of ancient Britain and in use before the Romans arrived. The name comes from the tribe of Iceni whose queen at one time was Boudicca. Here it creates the boundary between **Hertfordshire** and **Buckinghamshire**.

39 CHEDDINGTON (BR) The parish church of **St Giles's** is half a mile south of the station. The *L:r* small church contains fragments of the original Norman building: the tower was built in the 15th century.

40 MENTMORE The rooftops, some outbuildings *L:r* and the church of the estate of Mentmore are just visible in the clump of trees on the hillside about a mile from the line. Mentmore became well known when the contents were sold at auction for sèveral million pounds in 1978. The house became the 'seat of the World Government of the Age of Enlightenment' and the national centre of transcendental meditation. It was built in 1852–4 for Baron Meyer Amschel de Rothschild and designed by Joseph Paxton and his son in law G. H. Stoke. The mansion was sumptuously decorated and even had hot water heating and artificial ventilation. Paxton used the Jacobean style and there is much carved decoration outside and rich gilding inside the house.

The train crosses the boundary between **Bucking-hamshire** and **Bedfordshire**.

41 LEIGHTON BUZZARD (BR) The tall octa- *R:1* gonal spire of **All Saints** dominates the town. The church was consecrated by Bishop Oliver of Lincoln in 1288 and contains interesting graffiti and carvings. These is a precise drawing by a master-mason working on the building of a four-light window and also an illustration of the ancient 'Simon and Nellie' story in which Nellie threatens Simon with a spoon while she is baking a cake.

The church close to the station is **St Barnabas** *R:1* which was designed by Benjamin Ferrey and built in

All Saints, Leighton Buzzard

1848. The **station** is built of yellow and red bricks with simple brackets supporting the platform awnings.

Leighton Buzzard is apparently named after 'the tun belonging to a family nicknamed Buzzard, who grew leeks'. The town grew steadily throughout the 19th century but received a boost to the local sand industry during the First World War. Sand was used as ships ballast, and when imported supplies were cut off Leighton's industry benefited. In 1919 a 2-foot gauge light railway was opened to maintain the sand traffic and in the 1930s and again in the early 1950s 100,000 tons of sand were carried annually. Now a local preservation society looks after the light railway.

42 LINSLADE TUNNEL The Linslade tunnel is 285 yards long. It is the only curved tunnel on the line and cuts through blue clay and iron sandstone. There are three tunnels with the original in the centre, its portals decorated with battlements and turrets.

The Great Train Robbery, in which the London to Glasgow mail train was robbed, took place just north of the tunnel on 8 August 1963.

43 LINSLADE CHURCH The ancient market town of Linslade is now part of Leighton Buzzard. **St Mary's Church Linslade** is over a mile to the north. The church is built of yellow limestone and ironstone and has a 15th-century tower. Close beside it is the early 18th-century **manor farmhouse**. *R:l*

R:l

The train crosses the boundary between **Bedfordshire** and **Buckinghamshire**.

44 STOKE HAMMOND CHURCH St Luke's is *R:l*
built of ironstone with a Decorated central tower.
To the west are the masts of one of several
wireless transmitting stations in this area.   *L:r*

45 BLETCHLEY (BR) The chimneys of the **Lon-** *L:r*
don Brick Company kilns reveal where the
materials for this brick-built Victorian railway town
were made. Bletchley was heavily dependent on
the brick industry until the 1960s. Four million
bricks were produced a week and one quarter of
the population was employed by the company.
Bletchley developed from a small market to a
flourishing industrial town with the arrival of the
L&BR, the Bedford Railway in 1846 and the
Buckinghamshire Railway in 1850 and the establishment of the brick works. **St Mary's Church** was *L:r*
restored in the late 17th century by the antiquary
Brown Willis, who painted cherubs on the chancel
roof. He commemorated his parents with two plain
slabs on the church floor, unwilling to give them
'marble statues or fine Embellishments, whilst the
other part of God's house in which they lay wanted
a requisite Decency and Convenience'.

46 DENBIGH HALL BRIDGE Just over a mile
north of Bletchley Station the Denbigh Hall Bridge
carries the railway line over **Watling Street**,
(now the A5). Between April and September 1838
passengers on the L&BR had to leave the train at
Denbigh Hall and travel the next part of the
journey to Rugby by coach because the earthworks
in between were unfinished (see p. 16). There was
nothing more than an inn at Denbigh Hall. This was
on the site of a cottage where the Earl of Denbigh
had found refuge when caught in a snowstorm.

47 MILTON KEYNES (BR)   Milton Keynes is British Rail's newest station, opened in May 1982. The five platforms are linked by a covered overbridge. The platform buildings are covered in glistening cream tiles with clear plastic awnings. There are facilities for disabled passengers and ample car parking and a city bus network to the surrounding residential and industrial estates.

Milton Keynes began to grow after 1967 when 22,000 acres was designated for the city. The population is expected to be 200,000 by the 1990s. The station is part of Central Milton Keynes which contains the Borough Council headquarters, one of the largest shopping areas in Europe, a library, cafés, bars and restaurants. Some of the buildings have trees and shrubs inside them, others are built around courtyards, lawns and fountains. Cyclists and pedestrians have been specially provided for with their own network of Redways – reddish asphalt tracks – which cover the city's residential areas, industrial estates and parkland. The housing is particularly imaginative and varied and some of the brick and timber developments with tile or slate roofs can be seen from the train. The houses are grouped in various ways, some around courtyards, in crescents or squares, others in small mews or winding lanes. Most have gardens but every 'village' has a safe open space for children to play in. The Development Corporation prides itself on creating a city with fresh air, greenery and open spaces 'where the trees grow taller than the buildings'.

48 ST LAURENCE'S BRADWELL   was built in *R:1* about 1200 and has a west tower and a saddleback roof. On the other side of the line is a fragment of the 14th-century church belonging to **Bradwell**

MAP 3

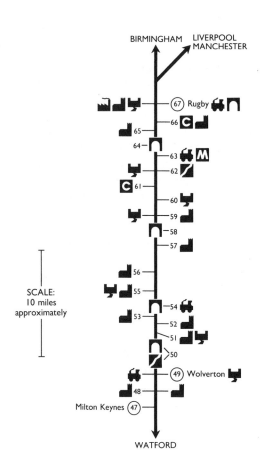

BIRMINGHAM

LIVERPOOL
MANCHESTER

67 Rugby

66

65

64

63

62

61

60

59

58

57

56

55

54

53

52

51

50

49 Wolverton

48

Milton Keynes 47

SCALE:
10 miles
approximately

WATFORD

Abbey. It looks like a small chapel all on its own in   L:r
a field. A Benedictine Priory was founded at
Bradwell c.1155 and given to Cardinal Wolsey by
Henry VIII at the Dissolution of the Monasteries.

49 **WOLVERTON** (BR)   South of Wolverton are   R:l
fibreglass sculptures of alarmingly lifelike black-and-
white cows standing in a field close to the railway
line. When the L&BR decided to develop Wolverton for their locomotive works it was only a hamlet
of 417 inhabitants, but by the end of the 19th
century some 5,000 men were employed in the
works. The works extend to the north and south
of the station, and one long **red-brick shed** before   L:r
the station still has camouflage colours from the
Second World War painted on the walls (now
Dunlop and Ranken Steel Service Centre). Houses
were built at Wolverton by the railway company
together with a church, schools and supplies of gas
and water. From 1854 housing developed to the
east of Wolverton, at **Bradwell**, as the original   R:l
landowner refused to sell any more of his land to
the company.

   Wolverton Station was rebuilt in 1881 and has
attractive red-brick platform buildings and an
immaculate white wooden footbridge. In the 1840s
Wolverton was famous for its refreshment rooms
which did good trade as every express train
stopped for ten minutes. Stout and Banbury cakes
were the favourites – 182,500 Banbury cakes were
consumed a year. Seven young ladies were employed as waitresses. 'As these youthful hand-
maidens stand in a row behind bright silver urns,
silver coffee pots, silver tea pots, cups, saucers,
cakes, sugar, milk, with other delicacies over which
they preside, the confused crowd of passengers,

simultaneously liberated from the train, hurry towards them with a velocity exactly proportionate to their appetite' (Sir Cusack P. Roney, *Rambles on Railways*, 1868).

50 WOLVERTON VIADUCT AND EMBANK-MENT The train crosses over the **River Great Ouse** on a viaduct 660 feet long, with six elliptical arches, each of 60 foot span. The viaduct is at the centre of an embankment 1½ miles long and 48 feet high. The canal company disputed the right of the L&BR to drive piles into the canal banks to build a temporary wooden bridge over the river while the embankment and viaduct were being constructed. Consequently Robert Stephenson and a team of navvies took advantage of Christmas Day festivities and erected a temporary bridge on 25 December 1834. On 30 December the canal company pulled it down and the case had to be settled in court with Chancery settling for the railway.

The embankment caused problems as well. It was composed partly of alum shale and this decomposed and then spontaneously combusted to the amazement of the locals: 'Dang it, they can't make this here railway arter all, and they've set it o' fire to cheat their creditors' (L. T. C. Rolt, *George and Robert Stephenson*).

51 CASTLETHORPE There was originally a station at Castlethorpe which is about 4 miles to the north of Wolverton. The parish church of **St Simon and St Jude** is close to the railway line. It *R:l* was built in the 13th–15th centuries but the tower had to be rebuilt after it collapsed in 1729. The **large stone farmhouse** between the church and *R:l* the line was built in the 17th century.

52 HANSLOPE CHURCH Nikolaus Pevsner described **Hanslope steeple** as the finest steeple in *R:l* Buckinghamshire. It rises to 180 feet and is a landmark for miles around. The original spire was built in the 15th century but was rebuilt after it was destroyed by lightning in 1804. The crockets decorating the ribs of the spire had a practical use. They provided a way for a brave volunteer to reach the weathercock in the event of its sticking.

Between Castlethorpe and Ashton the train crosses the boundary dividing **Buckinghamshire** from **Northamptonshire**.

53 ASHTON St Michael's Church close to the *L:r* line is basically medieval but the tower was built in 1848 to the design of R. C. Hussey. Inside is the earliest alabaster effigy in the county: of Sir John de Herteshull, who died c.1365. This is an area of rich pasture, dairy herds grazing on the gently undulating landscape and fields of vivid yellow rape (in May and June) providing a startling contrast to the luxurious greens of the meadows.

54 ROADE OR BLISWORTH CUTTING This mighty earthwork stretches 1½ miles between Roade and Blisworth. The digging caused Robert Stephenson and his team of navvies enormous problems (see p. 14) as they cut their way through the tons of limestone and clay with only gunpowder to assist their progress. About a mile away to the west and parallel to the cutting is an earlier marvel of engineering – the tunnel which carries the Grand Union Canal (formerly Junction) under the same ridge of hills from the valley of the Great Ouse to the valley of the Nene. The tunnel is perfectly straight, 3,075 yards 2 feet long, and took 11 years to dig.

Roade Station was at the south end of the cutting. It was closed in 1964. Roade was one of the rare villages not to be affected by the arrival of the railway. Between 1850 and 1930 the population remained static at about 700.

The **line to Northampton** leaves to the north *R:l* east. The cutting was deepened in 1875 when this line was opened.

55 BLISWORTH St John the Baptist has a *L:r* Perpendicular tower. The remains of the station at Blisworth can easily be spotted in front of the attractive yellow brick **Railway Hotel** which is *L:r* close to the line.

56 GAYTON There is a monument in **St Mary's** *L:r* **Church** (tower crowned with 4 pinnacles) to Francis Tanfield who died in 1558. The Tanfields built the 16th century **manor house** nearby.

57 BUGBROOKE St Michael's (decorated tow- *R:l* er with recessed spire) is a 13th-century church. Osborne, the Victorian author of popular railway guides, was disturbed by the name of the village which 'would, doubtless, be an object of romantic interest to the imaginative traveller if it were not for the associations which its name suggests, always unpleasing to persons going to or coming away from the World's Emporium'.

58 STOWE HILL TUNNEL The tunnel is 492 yards long and takes the train under Watling Street. The north entrance is embattled – the favourite Victorian design for tunnels.

59 WEEDON The parish church of **St Peter's** has *R:l* a Norman tower and is built of attractive yellow-orange stone. It is tucked between the railway line and the canal. In the churchyard there is a gravestone to 'Alice Old, widow' who lived, unbelievably, in the reigns of Elizabeth I, James I, Charles I, Charles II, James II and William and Mary, dying in 1691.

Weedon Barracks A large fortified depot *L:r* was built at Weedon in 1803 as a precaution against invasion by Napoleon. George III and his cabinet would be able to retreat to a safe place in the centre of England from where to direct operations. A branch canal was opened in 1804 to serve the depot and this entered the depot under two portcullises. The yellow-brick building which was part of George III's royal pavilion, the gatehouse complete with cupola and behind it the long ranges of red-brick and ironstone depot buildings have remained to this day, though the canal has been disused since c.1920.

60 BROCKHALL HALL The Elizabethan house *R:l* can just be seen in the trees on the hillside to the east. The owner, Thomas Reeve Thornton, gave the house a Gothick revamp in the early 19th century. He caused Robert Stephenson trouble over the route of the L&BR and forced him to deviate from his original line. Now the **M1**, the Grand Union Canal, the railway and the A5 all follow parallel routes in front of the hall.

61 DAVENTRY The **BBC Broadcasting Sta-** *L:r* **tion** about three miles to the west is close to Daventry. It is on Borough Hill, the site of an Iron Age hill fort which was used by the Romans for a villa. Excavations in 1972 revealed farm buildings and native huts from the first century AD. When the masts were erected relics were found of the camp of King Charles I's army, established in the last days of the Civil War. The Royalists received the news of Cromwell's arrival in the county at the camp on 12 June 1645 and two days later were defeated at the Battle of Naseby. The Empire Service was begun at the broadcasting station on 19 December 1932. During the Second World War the short-wave transmitters and aerials were increased at the station to broadcast the Voice of Britain to the world.

62 WHILTON There are six locks on the Grand Union Canal at Whilton. Narrowboats can be seen in **Whilton Marina**. **Whilton Lodge**, the large *R:l* white house west of the line, is beside Watling *L:r* Street and on the site of a Roman settlement known as Bannaventa, a walled town of 30 acres.

63 WATFORD GAP AND THE M1 The **red-** *R:l* **and black-brick engine house** marks the site of the original station at Watford. The **M1** motorway *R:l* is parallel to the railway line. The first section was opened on 1 November 1959.

64 KILSBY TUNNEL The Kilsby Tunnel is 2,423 yards long and was the most difficult work on the L&BR (see p. 14). Critics of the railway were horrified by the prospect of such a long deep tunnel and one proposed all locomotives should be fitted with a diaphragm, stiffened with whalebone, to promote ventilation in the depths. Stephenson consequently built two huge ventilation shafts 60 feet in diameter and over 100 feet deep, crowned with castellated towers. On one occasion, in April 1837, the navvies rioted and the militia were called from Weedon Barracks to restore order.

65 KILSBY VILLAGE Some 1,000 navvies camped L:r in and around the village of Kilsby while work proceeded underground. Their heavy drinking and enormous appetites caused much distress among the staid countryfolk. The parish church of **St Faith's** can be seen from the train. It has a L:r 13th-century tower with a small recessed spire.

The train crosses the boundary between **Northamptonshire** and **Warwickshire**.

66 HILLMORTON Just before **Hillmorton** R:l **Church** is the 900-acre site of the **GPO Radio Station** which played a vital role during the R:l Second World War. The church of **St John the Baptist** is below the line, and has a red ashlar R:l tower c.1300. The embankment which the train runs along was made out of material excavated from the Kilsby Tunnel.

67 RUGBY (BR) The disused **viaduct** (engineers R:l Charles Vignoles and Thomas Jackson Woodhouse) which can be seen crossing the Avon Valley to the north, used to carry the Midland Counties Railway to Leicester. The eleven 50 feet semi-elliptical arches are faced in blue engineering brick. The line is also crossed by a large cantilever bridge belonging to the Great Central Railway.

When the railway line was built passing close to **Rugby School** it was welcomed by the headmas- L:r ter Dr Thomas Arnold: 'I rejoice to see it and think that feudalism is gone for ever. It is so great a blessing to think that any one evil is really extinct.'

It was at Rugby School that the game of Rugby was invented in 1823. William Webb Ellis 'with a fine disregard for the rules of football as played in his time, first took the ball in his arms and ran with it'. William Butterfield designed the principal school buildings including the chapel (1872) whose octagonal central tower with a pyramid roof can be seen over the roof tops. There is a medallion in the chapel to the poet Rupert Brooke who was educated at Rugby and died in 1915 on the way to the Dardanelles. The tall stone spire belongs to the parish church of Rugby, **St Andrew's**, which was *L:r* also designed by William Butterfield in 1877–85.

Rugby Station presented Robert Stephenson with problems in the winter of 1833: 'The works at this point are at present in rather a backward state, owing to the severe and continuous frost, which has almost entirely put a stop to the brickwork and permanent road.' The present station is actually the third to be built. Rugby was constantly expanding in the 19th century with the arrival of more railway lines. The huge island platform with outer faces long enough to handle two main line trains at the same time was constructed in 1886. A massive wrought iron train shed spans the central concourse and buildings. Red-brick walls in an Italianate style enclose the tracks to the north and south. Unfortunately the station is in a dilapidated state – only a reflection of its past grandeur.

Rugby is dominated by the **GEC Works** and **Portland Cement**. The GEC has large factories on both sides of the track. The **Victorian** *L:r* **building in red brick** is adorned with a flamboyant red-brick tower. There are dozens of trading companies within the General Electric Company. Products made at Rugby include

MAP 4

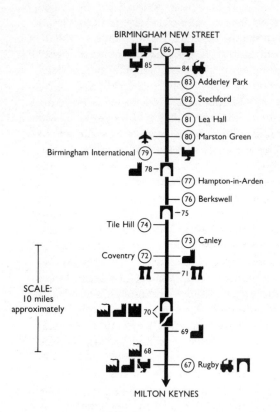

'complete power stations', motors and generators for mills, mining, oil rigs and steelworks, turbines, generation systems and auxiliary drives for ships, submarines, floating cranes and docks.

68 RUGBY PORTLAND CEMENT CO LTD *L:r*
The vast quarry below the railway line is an awesome sight as the train pulls out of Rugby (or approaches the town from the west).

69 CHURCH LAWFORD St Peter's is rock- *R:l* faced and was built in 1872 to the design of Slater and Carpenter. It is close to the **River Avon** which meanders to the north of the railway line. Church Lawford Cutting involved the removal of nearly ½ million cubic yards of earth which was used to make the Brandon Embankment to the west.

70 WOLSTON and BRANDON CASTLE
Wolston Priory is a large medieval house below *L:r* the line built of a mixture of materials. It is mostly of red sandstone but one side is of lias and two of the gables are timber-framed: the windows are mullioned. **St Margaret's Church** tower was *L:r* built in 1760 by Job Collins. The church is visible as the train crosses the 15-arch **viaduct** over the **River Avon**. On the west bank are the ruins of **Brandon Castle** which was built early in the 13th *L:r* century and has an oblong keep.

East of Coventry the train crosses between **Warwickshire** and the **West Midlands**.

71 CHEYLESMORE CEMETERY The cemetery *L&R* on the outskirts of Coventry, (now among housing estates and allotments) was laid out by Sir Joseph Paxton and opened in 1847. Paxton (the designer of the Crystal Palace) was MP for Coventry and there is a monument to him at the north entry to the cemetery, designed by Joseph Goddard.

72 **COVENTRY** (BR) Coventry is famous for three things: the ride of Lady Godiva, the bombing raids of the Second World War and Sir Basil Spence's Cathedral.

Coventry Station was designed by W. R. Headley, architect to the Midland Region of British Rail and built in 1959–62. The original station – which was one of few 19th-century stations to have a Ladies with a female attendant – had survived the bombing which destroyed so much of the city, but was demolished by British Rail. However, the new glass and concrete station, though unremarkable from the train, is clean and well laid out with a patio garden beside the waiting room.

Lady Godiva made her famous ride through the streets of Coventry to remit the heavy taxes imposed on the citizens by her husband Leofric 5th Earl of Mercia. Tennyson composed his poem on Godiva on a visit to Coventry:

I waited for the train at Coventry;
I hung with grooms and porters on the bridge,
To watch the three tall spires; and there I shaped
The city's ancient legend . . .

The **Cathedral of St Michael** was almost totally destroyed in a bombing raid on 14 November 1940. The steeple, however, survived, and was

Coventry Cathedral

used by Sir Basil Spence as part of his new
cathedral. This **blackened steeple** can be seen *R:l*
from the train rising 295 feet above the city. It was
built in 1371–1430: Ruskin described it reaching
'half-way to the sky'.

73 CANLEY (BR)   The old Standard Triumph production line was at Canley but it no longer
produces cars now, concentrating on research and
administration. The last car produced at Canley was
the TR7.

74 TILE HILL (BR)   The old Standard Triumph
paint shop at Tile Hill is now closed.

75 BEECHWOOD TUNNEL

76 BERKSWELL (BR)   The stations on this stretch
between Coventry and Birmingham were opened

for the local residents and are mostly very small, merely with platform shelters.

77 HAMPTON-IN-ARDEN (BR) Hampton-in-Arden is surrounded by rich farmland and is a popular place for wealthy Birmingham commuters to live. 'The village contains some cottages designed by W. E. Nesfield in the 1860s which are good early examples of the revival of interest in vernacular architecture in the late 19th century' (Alan Crawford).

78 BICKENHILL CHURCH The Perpendicular spire of **St Peter's** can be seen between the *L:r* bridges under the **M42** and under the A45(T).

79 BIRMINGHAM INTERNATIONAL (BR) Birmingham International Station was built to serve the National Exhibition Centre and is linked by a covered walkway and escalators. It is one of few major stations to be built since the war and has five platforms with platform buildings of yellow brick and brown tiles. The platform canopies are clad in purple-brown metal.

The **National Exhibition Centre** was *R* opened by the Queen in February 1976. The interconnected halls cover 11,840 square feet. The Metropole Hotel on the other side of Pendigo Lake from the railway line contains 18 banqueting and conference suites with air conditioning and equipment for multi-lingual translation in the meeting rooms. The International Arena, with bright orange girders rising from the roof, can seat up to 12,000. Delegates attending a convention in the arena can be provided with 'executive lunch trays' without even leaving their seats. All this is intended to create a vast money-making complex – Europe's most modern exhibition centre – attracting visitors from all over the world to exhibitions and conferences as well as giving the residents of Birmingham a new supply of entertainment with concerts, cabarets and restaurants.

The first British Telecom shareholders meeting was held in the exhibition centre in 1985.

80 MARSTON GREEN (BR)   This small local station with white wooden platform buildings decorated with curly brackets is at the north end of the runway of **Birmingham Airport**. The airport *L:r* was opened in July 1939 by the Duchess of Kent. Spring 1984 saw the opening of a new £50 million terminal building and apron. Plans to expand the airport were greeted with protests over the increase in noise from the local residents of Sheldon and Marston Green, and two vast landscaped noise barriers were built to screen neighbouring estates from the runways. An unusual method of communication between the airport and Birmingham International Station is the Maglev transit link. Cars, supported on a magnetic field, 'fly' about half an inch above an elevated track connecting rail and air services.

81 LEA HALL (BR)

82 STECHFORD (BR)   The station was opened in 1844 and within forty years an industrial estate had been established in the area. Houses began to be built in large numbers at the turn of the century and by 1930 all the once-agricultural land was covered to create a suburb of Birmingham.

83 ADDERLEY PARK (BR)

84 **CURZON STREET**   The L&BR terminated at Curzon Street until the growth in the volume of traffic necessitated the building of a bigger and much more central station at New Street (see below). Philip Hardwick designed the **grand entrance** for Curzon Street, a three-storey stone *R:l* block with four massive Greek Ionic columns designed as the answering monument to the Doric Arch at Euston. Unlike the Euston arch, the Curzon Street entrance has managed to survive and was sold a few years ago by BR to the City of Birmingham who are refurbishing it. Behind, though now unconnected with the entrance, is an enormous goods depot.

85 **GUN BARREL PROOF HOUSE**   Below the *L:r* line at the junction known as Proof House Junction is the Gun Barrel Proof House where guns made in Birmingham are still tested. The small brick building was designed in 1813 by John Horton and the handsome trophies above the central door were designed by William Hollins.

86 **BIRMINGHAM** (BR)   The **Rotunda**, a 24- *L:r* storey cylindrical building containing shops and offices, was designed by James A. Roberts and built in 1964–5. The tower is clad in fine white glass mosaic with aluminium sash windows and dominates the 3-acre Bull Ring Centre. The Bull Ring is the name of the market which has been held in Birmingham since the 12th century. The blackened spire belongs to **St Martin's in the Bull Ring**. *L:r* The sandstone church was originally built in the 13th century but – except for the tower and spire – it was rebuilt in 1873–5 by J. A. Chatwin in the style of the early 14th century. Bombing during the

Second World War destroyed much of Chatwin's work and the church was restored in 1957. Some of the stained glass is by Edward Burne-Jones and William Morris.

Birmingham's **Post Office Tower** is 500 feet *R:1* high and is a main link in the 'post office ultra high frequency micro wave television and telephone network'. Dish- and horn-type aerials are carried on the four circular concrete platforms.

Post Office Tower, Birmingham

Birmingham New Street The first station at New Street had a massive crescent-shaped train shed with a span of 211 feet supported by decorated brick walls and designed by E. A. Cowper. When George Borrow passed through on a holiday he commented, 'that station is enough to make one proud of being a modern Englishman'. Traffic grew, however, and the station became increasingly inadequate. In 1923 a dissatisfied traveller passed judgement: 'it is on a cold, wet night that the station reaches its most repulsive. It is ill-lit by a faulty gas system, devoid of adequate seating, the roof leaks in countless places, the lavatories proclaim their presence.' And in 1964 the former President of Birmingham's Chamber of Commerce declared 'I know of no other station in this country, Europe or the United States, which for filth, muck and severe dishevelment compares to New Street.' The result of decades of criticism was the demolition of the Victorian station and the erection of a vast and coldly efficient airport-like terminal which cost some £4½ million. Escalators take passengers up from the windy platforms to the concourse. Above the concourse is a large shopping centre. The main entrance to the station offers a glimpse of the concrete jungle which has engulfed a large part of the centre of Birmingham.

The **Stephenson Tower** is part of the complex, a tower-block of flats built around the chimney which serves the New Street boiler rooms. Although they were originally intended as council housing, British Rail found it more profitable to sell the flats to private individuals. However, these unfortunate residents have discovered the chimney has a disastrous effect on washing hanging from their balconies.

A Victorian traveller found Birmingham unattractive in 1851: 'There are few towns more uninviting than Birmingham; for the houses are built of brick toned down to a grimy red by smoke, in long streets crossing each other at right angles —

and the few modern stone buildings and blocks of houses seem as pert and as much out of place as the few idle dandies who are occasionally met among the crowds of busy mechanics and anxious manufacturers.' The smoke has cleared and it is now the 'few modern stone buildings' of the mid-19th century together with examples of later 19th-century city architecture which prevent Birmingham from succumbing totally to the concrete sterility of its station, shopping centre and car parks.

EUSTON
TO
LIVERPOOL

Euston to Watford (see pages 20-33)
Watford to Milton Keynes (see pages 34-44)
Milton Keynes to Rugby (see pages 45-53)

Introduction

Passengers travelling to Liverpool follow the original London and Birmingham Railway as far as Rugby (see p. 52). They then continue on the Trent Valley Railway which bypasses Birmingham, joining the original Grand Junction Railway line at Stafford. The Grand Junction Railway used to connect with the Liverpool and Manchester Railway at Earlestown to the west of Liverpool but a new line was laid via Runcorn which takes the train across the River Mersey on William Baker's girder bridge.

The Trent Valley Railway Company was founded in 1843 with Edward Watkins as Secretary: its aim to expand the industries already established in the Trent Valley. The first sod was cut in November 1845 by Sir Robert Peel, Prime Minister and MP for Tamworth (1830–50). He praised the self-sacrifice of the landowners: 'I assure them that there are many persons in this neighbourhood who have not scrupled to sacrifice private feeling and comfort, by consenting to their land being appropriated to the Trent Valley Railway. They have given consent from a conviction that this undertaking was one conducive to the public benefit, and that considerations of private interest should not obstruct the great one of the public good.' Nevertheless the owner of Shugborough Park was able to demand ornate entrances to the tunnel which the railway company dug under his estate.

The engineers for the line were Robert Stephenson and George Bidder and the contractor was Thomas Brassey. The line was opened in December 1847. The stations were designed by John William Livock, but many have been demolished. Tamworth and Lichfield have gone, also Stafford. The imaginative Jacobean-style building at Stafford was replaced by a 1960s functional design.

The Grand Junction Railway was opened on 4 July 1837 from Lime Street Station in Liverpool to a temporary terminus at Birmingham (Vauxhall). A scheme to link Birmingham with Birkenhead (the Mersey ferry-head to Liverpool) was discussed in Parliament as early as 1824 but opposed by landowners and canal-owners in Cheshire, the latter fearing – quite rightly – they would lose money. One canal agent from Nantwich was overheard by George Stephenson warning local farmers that the locomotive gave off breath as poisonous as a dragon's.

Joseph Locke surveyed the line which joined George Stephenson's Liverpool and Manchester Railway at Earlestown and from there had access to Liverpool or Manchester. It was not too expensive to build – £18,846 a mile as compared with Robert Stephenson's London and Birmingham Railway's £53,000. The opening was celebrated at Stafford by the Mayor firing a 21-gun salute with ancient cannon at the approach of 'Wildfire' pulling eight 1st class coaches – the first train to Birmingham.

With the threat of competition the Liverpool and Manchester Railway and the Grand Junction amalgamated to become the London and North Western Railway in 1846. Their headquarters were established at Crewe which was turned from a village into a thriving railway town in only a few years (see p. 88). Francis Webb, locomotive superintendant of the LNWR for 32 years, was largely responsible for building up Crewe. John Ramsbottom, famous for making the celebrated 'Lady of the Lake' class 2–2–2 express locomotive was also working at Crewe. Sir Cusack P. Roney honoured Ramsbottom in his *Rambles on Railways* (1868): 'one man who, if he had been in Egypt, with works not a quarter the size and not half so ably carried out, would have been at least a Bey, more probably a Pacha, in Austria a Count of the Holy

Empire; in any other country in the world, except England, with crosses and decorations, the ribbons of which would easily make a charming bonnet of existing dimensions. But in England the earnest, persevering, never tiring JOHN RAMSBOTTOM is John Ramsbottom – no more.'

MAP 5

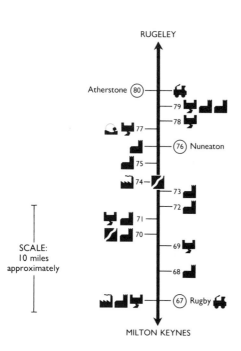

68 NEWBOLD ON AVON The red sandstone church of **St Botolph's** (Perpendicular tower) is in *R:l* the trees about half a mile from the line. The countryside around Newbold was fashionable in the 18th century because there was a spa at Newnham Regis nearby: 'The Air of this Country is exceeding Pleasant and Wholesome, the Sea being so remote that it is not infected with its noisome fumes' (*The Track of the Royal Scot*, LMS Route Book No 3).

69 NEWBOLD REVEL Newbold Revel (now St *R:l* Paul's College) at Stretton-under-Fosse is a red-brick mansion built for Sir Fulwar Skipwith in 1716. The architect was probably Francis Smith of Warwick and additions were made c.1900 by Edgar Wood. It is set in a park about a mile to the north of the line.

70 BRINKLOW is opposite Stretton-under-Fosse. There was a station for Brinklow beside the bridge which now carries the Fosse Way (A427) over the railway line. The parish church of **St John Baptist** *L:r* (Perpendicular tower) is about a mile from the line. A motte and bailey castle east of the church helped to guard the Fosse Way. There is a view of **Coventry** beyond the church (see p. 56). The *L:r* **Oxford Canal** flows beside the railway line *L:r* between Brinklow and Ansty. Both railway and canal pass under the **M6** to the north of Brinklow.

George Eliot described a journey through this countryside, 'watered at one extremity by the Avon, at the other by the Trent' in *Felix Holt*: 'As the morning silvered the meadows with their long lines of bushy willows marking the watercourses, or burnished the golden corn-ricks clustered near the long roofs of some midland home-stead, [one] saw the full-uddered cows driven from their pasture to the early milking.'

71 **ANSTY St James's** was mostly designed by *L:r* George Gilbert Scott in 1856 and has a small west tower with an octagonal bell-stage and spire. **Ansty Hall** is immediately next to the church. It is *L:r* built of red brick and has the date 1678 over the doorway. The top storey was added in 1800. Church and Hall are about half a mile from the line, situated beside the Oxford canal. But the **M69** (due to open Spring 1987) cuts through the pastoral landscape.

72 **SHILTON St Andrew's** with its Perpendicular *R:l* tower is next to the railway line close to where the station was originally sited and just before the line passes over the **M69**.

73 **BULKINGTON CHURCH St James's** has a *R:l* high 14th-century ashlar tower. Inside is a font made out of an antique Roman column. It was brought back by Richard Hayward of nearby Weston Hall (now a public house) as one of the spoils of his Grand Tour. Hayward was a talented sculptor and carved the bowl of the font. After his death the font was given to the church.

74 **BEDWORTH** is an industrial village with a *L:r* colliery and granite quarry and large crushing plant. The granite forms an unusual interruption in the red marl and sandstone scenery. It covers 7 square miles and has been extensively used for building. The colliery is at the north-eastern edge of the Warwickshire coalfield which extends over the

West Midlands plain. The line passes over the **Ashby de la Zouch Canal**, part of the network of canals which criss-crosses the Midlands and which helped to bring about the dramatic industrialisation of this part of Britain. George Eliot found the contrast between the industrial and rural pursuits of the region particularly striking: 'in these midland districts the traveller passed rapidly from one phase of English life to another: after looking down on a village dingy with coal-dust, noisy with the shaking of looms, he might skirt a parish all of fields, high hedges, and deep-rutted lanes.'

75 **ATTLEBOROUGH** The spire of **Holy Trinity** can be seen across the top of the houses. *L:r* Attleborough is now a suburb of Nuneaton. The population was expanding so rapidly at the beginning of the 19th century that the Earl of Harrowby gave the land on which to build Holy Trinity (designed by T. L. Walker and built in 1841–2 at a cost of £2,629).

76 **NUNEATON** (BR) Nuneaton was named after the Benedictine Nunnery founded in c.1155–60. From Norman times until the 1930s a curfew bell was rung nightly in the town. Nuneaton expanded rapidly in the late 18th and early 19th centuries with the coming of canals and then the railway. A variety of industries brought the town wealth and prosperity: the manufacture of bricks and tiles, hatting, clothing and spinning. George Eliot was born in 1819 at Arbury Farm, two miles to the south-west of Nuneaton; Arbury Mill became the setting for *The Mill on the Floss*.

　　St Nicholas has a large dark-grey stone *L:r* Perpendicular tower. There is a gruesome monument inside to Antony Trotman who died in 1703. A full-length skeleton lies in a winding sheet which is tied to the framework of the monument. It looks rather like the skeleton of Antony Trotman swaying in a hammock.

Nuneaton Station was re-built in 1909 and has a Neo-Georgian facade with circular windows and a clock tower. The red- and yellow-brick platform buildings and elaborate brackets supporting the awnings belong to the older Victorian station.

77 **TUTHILL WINDMILL** The base of Tuthill *L:r* Windmill can be seen on top of the **Hartshill Ridge** which overlooks Nuneaton. The ridge is made of ancient rocks – red and purple Cambrian shales and quartzites 5–6 million years old with diorite (an igneous rock) injected into them – on the edge of the Warwickshire coalfield. The quartzite and diorite are quarried for road-metal. Michael Drayton, the poet who composed 'Fair stood the wind for France' was born at Hartshill. He is thought to have become a page to Sir Henry Goodere of Polesworth. Goodere was a cousin of Sir Philip Sidney and friend of John Donne, who wrote his poem 'Good Friday' on leaving Polesworth in 1613.

78 **CALDECOTE HALL** was designed in 1879–80 *R:l* by R. J. and J. Goddard in red brick in a Jacobean style and cost over £21,000.

79 **WITHERLEY AND MANCETTER St** *R:l* **Peter's**, Witherley is over a mile from the line beside the **River Anker** and just into **Leicestershire**. In 1924 the spire was struck by lightning and

crashed through the nave. It cost £5,500 to restore in 1926. **St Peter's**, Mancetter is closer to the line *R:l* and has a Perpendicular tower. The **Manor House** (timber framed c.1330) is between the church and the railway line. There was a Roman settlement at Mancetter called Manduessedum.

80 ATHERSTONE (BR)   is an ancient stronghold of the hatting industry. The local firm of Messrs Wilson and Stafford became well known during the Second World War for making most of the bush hats used by the troops in Burma and the Far East.

    Atherstone Station has a particularly attrac- *R:l* tive Tudor-style station house of diapered red brick. It was designed by J. W. Livock but is no longer used by BR. A **large sign** just south of the *R:l* station declares '102 miles to London': it is attached to a red brick building.

81 MEREVALE HALL   looks like a castle with its *L:r* embattled towers and walls, magnificently sited on the hill side west of Atherstone. It is actually a Victorian house, designed in the Gothic–Elizabethan style by Edward Blore in 1838–44. Merevale is the home of the Dugdales, descendants of Sir William Dugdale (1605–86), the compiler of the *Monasticon*, an account of English monastic houses. The fragments of Merevale Abbey, a Cistercian house founded in 1148 by Robert Earl Ferrers, are in the park. Blore's employer was William Stratford Dugdale MP, a Tory landowner with very decided ideas about his workers. The first workers he hired were members of the union and went on strike. They were instantly sacked by Dugdale: 'by September I collected another set of workmen who conformed to my rules and not to

MAP 6

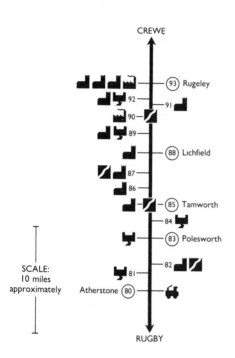

CREWE

93 Rugeley

92

91

90

89

88 Lichfield

87

86

85 Tamworth

84

83 Polesworth

82

81

Atherstone 80

SCALE:
10 miles
approximately

RUGBY

those of the Union – we had no more trouble with them during all the time the house was building.' There was no central heating and only one bathroom at Merevale. Blore's ex-pupil Henry Clutton designed the lodge gateway in 1848–9.

82 **GRENDON CHURCH** The stately tower of *R:l* Grendon Parish Church was added in 1845 by R. C. Hussey to the much older medieval church. Inside are monuments to the Chetwynds, an important landowning family in the area who lived at Grendon Hall and Pooley Hall. The **Coventry Canal** and the **River Anker** flow between the railway line *R:l* and the church.

83 **POLESWORTH** (BR) Immediately after Poles- worth Station is **Pooley Hall**, a large brick *L:r* mansion said to have been built in 1509 by Sir Thomas Cokayne. Pooley Hall gave its name to the nearby colliery which was one of the first to adopt the principle of direct conversion of coal into electricity. At one time the colliery lighted all the houses within a radius of 5 miles.

West of Polesworth the train crosses the boundary between **Warwickshire** and **Staffordshire**.

84 **AMINGTON HALL** is the large Georgian *R:l* ashlar-faced mansion about a mile to the north.

85 **TAMWORTH** (BR) Tamworth is famous for its pigs, pork pies and pasties, as well as being the birthplace of Sir Robert Peel, Prime Minister under both William IV and Queen Victoria. The town centre is to the south of the station with the earthworks of a Norman castle, the medieval parish

church of **St Editha** and the Town Hall built by *L:r*
Thomas Guy, founder of Guys' Hospital in London.

Tamworth Station was one of J. W. Livock's
finest achievements but it was rebuilt to serve one
of Britain's busiest mail exchange points. The train
crosses the **River Anker** just to the east of the
station.

86 **HOPWAS** Hopwas Hays Wood (now partly *L:r*
taken over by the Ministry of Defence for firing
ranges) is on the other side of the **River Tame**. **St
Chad's**, Hopwas is a very small church on the
south side of the wood over a mile from the
railway line. It was built in 1881 by John Douglas
and has a shingled spirelet on top of the tower. The
base is of brick but the upper parts are timber
framed.

87 **WHITTINGTON CHURCH** **St Giles's** has a *L:r*
medieval tower with a later spire.

The **Coventry Canal** can be seen at Whittington.
It is to the west of the line; then the line crosses
over the canal, just before going under the A38 and
into Lichfield.

88 **LICHFIELD** (BR) The railway-guide writer
George Measom was hardly fair to Lichfield when
he wrote in the mid-19th century: 'though Lichfield
will repay the traveller for spending a few hours in
examining the buildings and monuments . . . yet the
city will appear intolerably dull, and he will be glad
to return to the station and good-looking red brick
building.' Livock's station has recently been demolished but at least some of the fine Georgian
houses of Lichfield have survived. Dr Johnson was

born in the city in 1709. His father was a bookseller and his house is now a museum. Johnson was immortalised in his biography written by James Boswell. His most famous work was his *Dictionary of the English Language*, first published in 1755. Erasmus Darwin was also born in Lichfield and his 18th-century house is still standing. Darwin was a physician and scientist and the grandfather of Charles Darwin. He wrote the prophetic poem 'The Botanic Garden':

> Soon shall thy arm, Unconquered Steam, afar
> drag the slow barge, or drive the rapid car;
> Or on wide waving wings expanded bear the
> flying chariot through the fields of air.

The Lichfield Heritage Centre, opposite Samuel Johnson's house, gives an insight into the town's history.

Lichfield Cathedral is easily distinguished by its *L:r* three spires known as 'the ladies of the Vale'. It was badly damaged by the Roundheads during the Civil War after the Royalists fortified it. The central spire was destroyed and lead was torn from the roof. Since then the cathedral has been extensively restored by James Wyatt (1788–95), Sydney Smirke (1842–6), George Gilbert Scott (1857) and John Oldrid Scott. Inside the cathedral is St Chad's Gospel (St Chad was the first bishop), an illuminated manuscript codex.

89 HANCH HALL is close to the railway line and *L:r* surrounded by trees. It is easily distinguished by the blue-painted woodwork and small bell tower. One of the rooms in the house has early 16th-century timbers and another was a Victorian ball room.

Lichfield Cathedral

In the distance is the tower of **St James's,** *L:r* **Longdon**. George Eliot described the hedgerows which still surround the fields and border the railway line: 'liberal homes of unmarketable beauty – of the purple-blossomed ruby-berried nightshade, of the vivid convulvulus climbing and spreading in tendrilled strength till it made a great curtain of pale-green hearts and white trumpets.'

90 ARMITAGE The railway line passes between *L:r*
the **Trent and Mersey Canal** and the **River
Trent**. The enormous factory close to the line is
owned by Armitage Shanks 'better bathrooms'.
The building of canals in the Midlands in the second
half of the 18th century did more than boost
industry and commerce. Agriculture also benefited
and the standard of living of ordinary people was
improved: 'the cottage, instead of being half
covered with miserable thatch, is now covered
with a substantial covering of tiles or slates,
brought from the distant hills of Wales or Cumber-
land. The fields, which before were barren, are
now drained and by the assistance of manure,
conveyed on the canal toll-free, are clothed with a
beautiful verdure. Places which rarely knew the use
of coal are plentifully supplied with that essential
article upon reasonable terms' (Thomas Pennant,
1782).

91 MAVESYN RIDWARE CHURCH St Nich- *R:l*
olas has a Perpendicular tower. Inside is the
Mavesyn Chapel containing a monument to Sir
Robert Mavesyn who died fighting for Henry IV at
the Battle of Shrewsbury in 1403.

92 ARMITAGE PARK (HAWKESYARD PRIORY) *L:r*
AND ST JOHN'S CHURCH Armitage Park is
a pinnacled and battlemented Gothic stuccoed
house built in 1760 by Nathaniel Lister. It was
bought by Mrs Josiah Spode (widow of the famous
potter who died in 1827 leaving a fortune) in 1839
and renamed Hawkesyard by her son Josiah Spode
IV. He left the house to Dominican monks on his
death in 1893. They employed E. Goldie to design
their priory (1896–1914) behind the house, but still

use the 18th-century house for retreats and conferences. **St John's Church** is situated on a *L:r* rock above the **River Trent** some distance behind the priory. The short tower was built in 1632 and the rest of the church is in the Norman style, built in 1844–7 to the design of a Stafford architect called Henry Ward.

93 RUGELEY (BR) The **power station** before *L:r* Rugeley Station was opened in 1963. Three churches can be seen from the line. The spire belongs to the Roman Catholic church of **St Joseph and St Ethelreda** and was designed by Charles Hansom in 1849–50. The towers belong to *L:r* the old medieval **St Augustine** and the 19th- and 20th-century **St Augustine** (with the larger tower).

Rugeley was given unwelcome publicity in the mid-19th century over the gruesome practices of Dr Palmer who murdered his wealthy patients with strychnine. The townsfolk were so upset by their notoriety that a deputation was sent to Palmerston asking him to change the name of the town – to no avail.

Rugeley Power Station

MAP 7

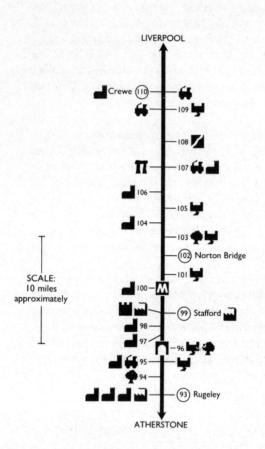

LIVERPOOL

Crewe ⑩

⑨ Norton Bridge

Ⓜ

⑨ Stafford

⑨ Rugeley

SCALE:
10 miles
approximately

ATHERSTONE

94 CANNOCK CHASE is practically all that re- *L:r* mains of the great forest which once covered Staffordshire. The heath and woodland grows on the dry sandy soils of the Bunter Sandstone which crosses the Midland plain. The area has remained uncultivated because of its impractical nature and is now preserved as a place of recreation.

95 COLWICH The attractive limestone **station-** *L:r* **house** of Colwich survives beside the line. It is one of the few remaining stations designed by John William Livock in 1847 for the Trent Valley Railway and has his distinctive gables and diamond tiles.

St Michael's Church has a high west tower *L:r* built in 1640. Inside the church are monuments to the Anson, Sparrow and Wolesley families. Lord George Anson was a celebrated admiral and circumnavigator and his fortune – made capturing Spanish treasure galleons – was used by his brother Thomas to improve Shugborough House and Park (see below). Sir William Wolesley drowned in his carriage when the mill dam suddenly burst in a thunderstorm in 1728. The four horses were also drowned but the coachman was carried to an orchard and hung on to an apple tree until the waters fell.

St Mary's Abbey was built c.1825 as Mount *R:l* Pavilion by Viscount Tamworth, son of the 7th Earl Ferrers. It is in the Tudor Gothic style with a castellated front. A Benedictine order of contemplative nuns moved into the mansion in 1834.

The line divides immediately after Colwich: to the west is the line to Stafford, Crewe and Liverpool, to the north the line to Macclesfield, Stockport and Manchester.

96 SHUGBOROUGH TUNNEL Shugborough Tunnel is 776 yards long and has distinctive ornamental portals designed by J. W. Livock to the satisfaction of the owner of Shugborough. The tunnel was the largest engineering work on the Trent Valley Railway and its flamboyant entrances earned it the nickname the 'Gates of Jerusalem'. Livock also had to decorate the Lichfield Drive Bridge (with sea horses and lions) so that the railway could cross the park.

There is a brief glimpse of **Shugborough Park** R:l **and House**. Shugborough Hall was built in 1693 for William Anson and enlarged in the 18th century by his grandson Thomas who also filled the park with the buildings designed by James 'Athenian' Stuart. Thomas Anson was a founder member of the Society of Dilettanti which sent Stuart to Athens to draw the principal buildings. These provided the inspiration for the Arch of Hadrian, the Tower of the Winds, the Doric Temple and the Lantern of Demosthenes. The 2nd Lord Lichfield inherited the property in 1854. The present Lord Lichfield occupies a flat in the house which is now owned by the National Trust and open to the public. The Staffordshire County Museum is housed in a stable block and Shugborough Park Farm, the old home farm of the estate, is now a working museum of farming.

97 WALTON ON THE HILL CHURCH St L:r **Thomas's** was designed by Thomas Trubshaw and built in 1842. The tower has a recessed spire.

98 BASWICH CHURCH Holy Trinity has a L:r medieval tower with an 18th-century top.

99 STAFFORD (BR) is approached from the east along the **Queensville Curve** which gives a fine view of the town. The expansion of Stafford in recent years is clearly revealed by the extensive new housing on both sides of the line. Stafford has been a prosperous town since the Middle Ages when wool and cloth were the chief industries. In the late-18th century shoemaking became important (the Lotus Boot Factory was established close to the station) followed by the production of table salt. Brine was discovered by accident when the corporation was sinking a bore-hole to provide a fresh water supply for the town. Engineering then became important with the Castle Locomotive Works of W. G. Bagnall Ltd and a large **GEC** *R:1* **factory** where diesel engines, earthquake testing equipment and transformers are some of the products. Research and development of new engineering materials is also carried out; microchemical, spectrographic, X-ray and electron microscopy techniques are used in the laboratories. Opposite the GEC factory are the works of BRC – **British Reinforced Concrete.** *L:r*

Stafford Station used to be Livock's Jacobean-style building, built in 1843–62, but this was demolished and replaced with a functional, far less characterful station in 1961–2, designed by W. R. Headley, architect to the Midland Region of BR. Dickens commented on the decline of the coaching inn in Stafford after the arrival of the railway: 'The extinct town inn, the Dodo ... possesses interminable stables at the back ... horseless.'

Stafford Castle can be seen on top of the hill *L:r* to the west of the town, almost engulfed by trees. The Normans erected a motte and bailey castle on the site and this was used by Ralph de Stafford in

1348 to build a new fortification. The Roundheads besieged the castle during the Civil Wars and it was eventually demolished in 1643 though Lady Stafford put up a valiant defence. Sir George Jerningham, later Lord Stafford, reconstructed the castle in c.1817 but little now remains.

100 SEIGHFORD CHURCH The 17th-century *L:r* brick tower of **St Chad's** decorated with Gothic pinnacles (1748) can be seen just after the train passes under the **M6**.

101 SHALLOWFIELD AND IZAAK WALTON'S *R:l* **COTTAGE** The small timber-framed and whitewashed cottage (open to the public) is easily missed. It is below the line, only a short distance away and on its own close to a road bridge over the railway. The cottage was built in about 1600. Izaak Walton did not live in it, but gave the cottage and the rest of his Halfhead Farm Estate to the town of Stafford to be used for charitable purposes. The cottage was opened as a museum in 1924 and the original thatched roof replaced by tiles after a fire in 1939.

102 NORTON BRIDGE (BR)

103 MEECE BROOK is where Piscator drew in- *R:l* spiration and fished in Izaak Walton's *The Compleat Angler*. It meanders close to the railway line for some miles north of Norton Bridge. Beyond the river to the east are the trees of **Swynnerton Park**, the estate of Lord Stafford.

On the hillside about 1½ miles east of the line is a magnificent **water tower**. The yellow- and red- *R:l* brick square tower has giant arches supporting the water tank. It is part of the system providing water for the Five Towns over the hills to the east.

104 STANDON CHURCH **All Saints** is opposite *L:r* Swynnerton Park on the west side of the line. The tower dates from the 14th century and the church was restored by George Gilbert Scott in 1846–7.

105 HATTON PUMPING STATION This is a *R:l* splendid example of Victorian industrial architecture. The yellow- and red-brick buildings were erected in 1890–98 and include a tall chimney and a central building with an Italianate tower. Inside are Corinthian columns. The water-bearing stratum beneath the surface is known as the Bunter Bed.

106 CHAPEL CHORLTON The medieval tower *L:r* of **St Laurence's Church** was remodelled by James Trubshaw Junior in 1826–7.

107 MADELEY There used to be a station for *R:l* Madeley village which is to the east of the line. The church of **All Saints** has a Perpendicular tower *R:l* and some of the stained glass is by William Morris, Edward Burne-Jones and Ford Madox Brown. With sharp eyes you may spot the **monument** marking *L:r* the 12 allotments and fountain erected by Lady Houghton, sister of the 3rd Baron Crewe (see Crewe Hall p. 88) in 1850, in memory of her aunt and as a gift to the poor.

108 BETLEY MERE There are meres – small lakes *R:l* – dotted throughout this part of the country. The largest is 156 acres. They were formed as a result of the extensive salt working in the red marl of the

Cheshire Plain. The salt occurs in the red marl in beds with an average thickness of 100 feet. Extraction has caused the surface to subside thus creating the meres which are usually surrounded by reeds and birch trees.

The train crosses between **Staffordshire** and **Cheshire**.

109 **CREWE HALL**   About a mile south of Crewe Station, the train passes **Basford Hall Sidings**. *L:r* Across the fields to the east and almost hidden by a large clump of trees is **Crewe Hall**. It is just *R:l* possible to see the tower appearing above the treetops. The original Crewe Hall was built by Sir Randolph Crewe in 1615–36. The 3rd Baron Crewe employed Edward Blore to restore the house in 1830–40. Blore spent £30,000 but his work was destroyed by fire in 1866. E. M. Barry rebuilt the hall giving it the ornate tower with four chimneys disguised as pinnacles.

110 **CREWE** (BR)   When the Grand Junction Railway arrived at Crewe in 1837 the population was about 200, living in small farms and cottages. By 1842, however, the station was the focus of four railway lines and the locomotive works which had been moved from Edge Hill were about to begin production. The railway company built houses, churches and schools and by 1851 the population had risen to 4,571. The salary of the curate and the schoolmaster were paid by the company which also provided a doctor and two policemen, organised the supply of mains water, the emptying of ash pits, cess pools and privies, and even set up a savings bank for their employees. Four classes of houses

MAP 8

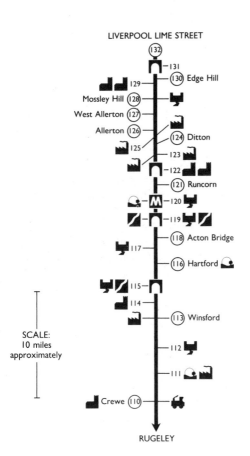

were built: 'first, the villa-style lodges of the superior officer; next a kind of ornamental Gothic constitutes the house of the next in authority; the engineers domiciled in detached mansions, which accomodate four families, with gardens and separate entrances; and last the labourer delights in neat cottages of four apartments, the entrances within ancient porches.' (1846).

Crewe Station consists of three broad island platforms each with creamy-yellow brick buildings decorated with red and dark blue brick dressings, all under a lateral train shed. The bay windows have Greek heads on the keystones. Immediately next to the station is the **Crewe Arms**, built in the R:/ Jacobean style and opened in 1837. It was taken over by the LNWR as their railway hotel in 1864. Rather less decorative is the 13-storey block by the station which is **Rail House**, designed by F. S. Curtis and R. C. Moorcroft, British Rail architects, and erected in 1967–8.

The parish church of **Christ Church** is close to L:r the line, north of the station. It was paid for by the Grand Junction Railway and begun in 1843. The architect was probably John Cunningham of Liverpool who also designed the first railway cottages at Crewe. The tower was designed by J. W. Stansby, engineer on the railway company staff and added in 1877. It was originally finished with an iron crown made at the railway workshops.

III The countryside to the north of Crewe is flat – mostly dairy pastures on top of the vast **CHESHIRE SALTFIELD**. The saltfield has been worked by the Ancient Britons, the Romans and up to the present day. The chief towns on the field – Nantwich, Northwich, Middlewich – share the same last syllable which means white. The saying 'worth your salt' was from Roman soldiers being paid with salt instead of money. In Saxon times salt was taxable and Domesday Book records the unusual laws of the area: 'whoever committed an offence within these bounds could atone for it by paying 2s. or 30 boilings of salt, except for homicide or theft, for which the offender was adjudged to death.' Sources of salt are the brine springs and mines of rock salt. Now the salt is made into the chief alkalis of commerce including soda and bleaching powder. ICI Alkali is at Northwich (one of the birthplaces of the chemicals industry in Britain) and United Alkali (now ICI) at Widnes. The wealth of the area is revealed by the fine farm-houses and manor houses to be seen from the line.

12 **LEA HALL** at Wimboldsley is an attractive *R:l* 18th-century red-brick house with a half-timbered barn.

13 **WINSFORD** (BR)   Winsford is the headquarters of **ICI Salt Ltd**. The country's largest rock salt *L:r* mine is here. In the mid-19th century there were '25 salt works here, some of them being like little towns in extent'. The chimneys belonged to the open fires over which the brine was evaporated in large pans. Almost all the working population of the town were employed in the salt industry which was given an important boost with the arrival of the railway. Winsford Station was rebuilt in the 1960s for the electrification of the line and the platform buildings are in the mustard yellow colour which is common to all contemporary stations on this route to Liverpool.

114 OVER CHURCH St John the Evangelist *L:r* (thin broach spire) was built in 1860–3 by John Douglas for his early patron Lord Delamere.

Over, Winsford, Swanlow and Wharton are all involved in the salt and chemicals industries. Over is also the birthplace of Robert Nixon, the 'Cheshire Prophet'. The predictions of this illiterate plough-boy are part of local folklore.

115 VALE ROYAL AND THE WEAVER *L:r* **VIADUCT** The **River Weaver** is close to the railway line, though often hidden by the sides of the cuttings. It flows through the ancient estate of Vale Royal Abbey. The Abbey was founded by Edward I and consecrated by the Bishop of St Asaph in 1277. The King, Queen Eleanor and their son Alphonso laid the first stones. When only a Prince, Edward had been caught in a storm returning from the Crusades and vowed that if he was saved he would raise an Abbey. The remains are now covered up but a house was built on the site by Sir Thomas Holcroft after the Dissolution of the Monasteries. The house passed to the Cholmondeleys – Lords of Delamere – until 1947 and then became the headquarters of the Cheshire Constabulary. The inside of the house was fashionably gothicised in c.1800 and Edward Blore added a clock turret and gables.

The gothic gables of **Vale Royal** can just be *L:r* seen in the trees as the train crosses over the **Weaver Viaduct**. One of the first railway writers, E. C. Osborne, described the magnificent view from the centre of Joseph Locke's viaduct soon after it was opened in 1837: '70 feet above the water, high in air, and midway between the two arms of the valley. The hall or abbey, nearly hid amongst the luxuriant foliage around, gleams through the vista in the distance – the river moves slowly on, bearing on its surface the stately barge, or still larger and loftier vessel; – the solitary traveller through the Vale winds his way along the devious path, and the glorious hills and woods bound the scene, as an everlasting barrier against all encroachment.'

16 **HARTFORD** (BR) Just north of the station, the train passes under the railway line between Chester and Manchester which marks the edge of the Vale Royal Abbey lands. A field just beside the line is called **Gibbet Hill** after the local gibbet erected *R:l* to deal with unfortunate offenders.

17 **WEAVERHAM HOSPITAL** Part of Grange Hospital, Weaverham, is **Hefferstone Grange**, a *L:r* fine brick manor house, built in 1741, with a stable block adorned with a cupola. In front are the green huts, part of the hospital complex.

18 **ACTON BRIDGE** (BR)

19 **DUTTON VIADUCT** Immediately north of the viaduct is the attractive half-timbered and red-brick **Dutton Lodge Farm**. The Dutton *R:l* Viaduct is ¼ mile long, 65 feet above the water, 25 feet wide and has 20 arches each with a span of 65 feet. The views to the east and west are magnificent with the **Weaver Navigation** and the old course of the **River Weaver** passing underneath.

20 **NORTON WATER TOWER** After passing *R:l* over the **M56** there is a good view of Norton Water Tower. This ornate tower with a pierced

base was built c.1890–2 for Liverpool Corporation and designed by the municipal water engineer G. F. Deacon. To the south west are the **Frodsham and Helsby Hills** which form a dramatic 'edge' to *L:r* the flat valley of the **River Mersey**.

121 **RUNCORN** (BR) The station is approached from the south through a rocky cutting. It is in the same mustard-yellow painted metal and concrete as the other 1960s post-electrification stations on this line.

In the 16th century Runcorn was no more than 'a poor townlet by a salt creke'. It only began to expand when the Bridgewater Canal was extended to the town in 1773. The opening of the railway bridge across the Mersey in 1869 dramatically improved the town's communications and consequent residential and industrial development. In 1964 Runcorn was given a further boost with the establishment of the Runcorn Development Corporation. Its aim was to provide additional employment and housing for people in the North Merseyside area. The chief architect was F. Lloyd Roche who has planned for an eventual population of 90,000.

122 **CROSSING THE RIVER MERSEY** The road and rail bridges dominate Runcorn to the south and Widnes to the north. The **railway bridge** was designed by William Baker and consists of three lattice girder spans of 305 feet, built up piece by piece on the spot. It is approached from Ditton Junction to the north on a viaduct of 59 arches rising to a height of 75 feet. Work began on the bridge in April 1864 and the first passenger train crossed on 1 April 1869. The bridge was given a

flamboyant Gothic look but the embattled towers are now sadly soot-blackened. It shortened the distance between Crewe and Liverpool by over 8 miles.

Immediately next to Baker's bridge is the eau de nil **road bridge** designed by Mott, Hay and Anderson and built in 1956–61. The roadway hangs from a single steel arch with a span of 1,082 feet – the third largest steel arch in the world when the bridge was built.

All Saints, Runcorn   Below the bridges on *R:l* the south bank is All Saints, a red-stone church built in the Early English style with a high steeple. It was designed by Salvin and erected in 1847–9.

St Mary's, Widnes   On the north bank is St *R:l* Mary's, a large red-stone church with a substantial tower, built in 1908–10 and designed by Austin and Paley.

23 WIDNES WEST BANK   Since John Hutchinson *L&R* established his soda factory in Widnes in 1847 the town has become a centre for the chemical industries (ICI). Widnes West Bank was planned with a grid layout in the 1860s and 1870s. The Hutchinson's Estate of 1862 provided housing for workers on one of the first industrial estates in the country. A promenade was provided along the riverside for recreation.

24 DITTON (BR)   Travelling away from Liverpool there is a fine view of the bridges over the Mersey as the line curves from Ditton Junction down to Widnes. Before the railway bridge was built across the Mersey, the main line from London to Liverpool continued north from Acton Bridge to Earlestown and then turned westwards along the original Liverpool and Manchester Railway. The line from Ditton to Halewood and Speke was part of the St Helens Railway absorbed by the LNWR in 1864.

125 The **FORD MOTOR WORKS** at **HALE-** *L&* **WOOD** began production in 1963. The works cover 365 acres and are the second largest complex in Britain (the largest is at Dagenham) producing Escort cars, vans and estates.

126 **ALLERTON** (BR) The railway line from Speke via Allerton to Edge Hill was opened by the LNWR on 15 February 1864. In the 19th century Allerton was not a suburb of Liverpool but a popular country retreat for some of the richest merchants of the city where they built mansions designed by leading architects of the day. Some of the houses have survived though they are not visible from the train. The plantation-owner William Shand and the colliery-owner J. Grant Morris employed Alfred Waterhouse. The cotton merchant Joseph Leather employed George Gilbert Scott and Tate the sugar refiner built two houses designed by Norman Shaw.

127 **WEST ALLERTON** (BR; 1939)

128 **MOSSLEY HILL** (BR) About a mile north of Mossley Hill Station is **Wavertree School**, a fine *R:1* red- and black-brick Victorian school with central tower, clearly visible across the playing fields.

129 **THE CATHEDRALS OF LIVERPOOL** As *L:r* the train crosses **Wavertree Junction** there is a good view across the slate roofs of Liverpool of the two cathedrals. The more conventional Gothic-

style building in red sandstone is Anglican; the circular building with its unusual lantern is Roman Catholic.

Sir Giles G. Scott won the competition for the Anglican Cathedral in 1903 but redesigned it in 1910–11. It was still not finished when he died in 1960 but was consecrated by the Queen on 25 October 1978. The tower rises 331 feet above the city and is particularly impressive from the graveyard below. Scott developed the Gothic style 'to something original and modern, monumental and sublime, yet delicate and romantic' (Gavin Stamp, *Britain in the Thirties*).

The Catholic Cathedral was originally to be designed by Lutyens but only the crypt was built when work was abandoned in 1940. Frederick Gibberd won the competition to complete the cathedral in 1960 and built on top of Lutyens's

Roman Catholic Cathedral, Liverpool

crypt. The cathedral is 194 feet in diameter and on top is a fully glazed lantern weighing 2,000 tons crowned with pinnacles rising to 290 feet. The stained glass in the lantern is by John Piper and Patrick Reyntiens. The whole building cost £1½ million.

130 EDGE HILL (BR)   The main line to London joins the Liverpool to Manchester line just east of Edge Hill Station in a maze of junctions, sidings, signals, cables and soot-blackened walls. Olive Mount Cutting is east of Edge Hill but the dramatic steep-sided cutting has been widened to take additional tracks. The *Liverpool Mercury* for 10 August 1827 described the first recorded death of a railway navvy at Edge Hill: 'the poor fellow was in the act of undermining a heavy head of clay, 14 or 15 feet high, when the mass fell upon him, and literally crushed his bowels out of his body.'

Edge Hill Station was opened in 1836 in time for the inaugural service to Birmingham on the Grand Junction Railway. The station expanded over the years to include a goods depot, the Grand Junction Railway's locomotive works and the associated sidings, yards and marshalling yards. The original red sandstone buildings designed by John Cunningham were restored for the 150th anniversary of the Liverpool and Manchester Railway.

131 TUNNELS INTO LIVERPOOL LIME STREET   The train approaches Lime Street Station through a series of tunnels – Overbury Street, Mount Pleasant and Russell Street – and under several bridges. There are glimpses of high rocky walls covered with wet lichen and ferns above the track.

The tunnel under Liverpool was the first of the great Victorian railway tunnels and dug for the Liverpool and Manchester Railway. It is 1¼ miles long and gave employment to 300 miners. Four men were killed during the excavations which proved harder than expected. The pilot tunnel ran 13 feet out of true in places. 'Unexpected veins of soft blue shale and quicksand threatened to drown the workings and water made it difficult to build masonry lining.' The more daring Liverpool citizens descended one of the 60 feet shafts in a bucket to watch the work in progress: 'some infernal operation in the region of Pluto'.

132 LIVERPOOL (BR)   Liverpool began to expand at the end of the 17th century with the trade in sugar, tobacco and cotton from the West Indies and Virginia. It was the slave trade, however, which brought greater wealth from the beginning of the 18th to the beginning of the 19th centuries. Daniel Defoe, visiting the town in 1724–7, wrote 'no town in England, except London, ... can equal Liverpoole for the Fineness of the Streets and Beauty of the Buildings.' Slaves laid the foundations for Liverpool's golden age as England's prime Atlantic port, picking the cotton that was brought to the factories of Lancashire and turning some of the citizens into millionaires. The extraordinary Royal Liver Building, designed by W. Aubrey Thomas (1908–10) and the Dock Office Building by Arnold Thornely reflect the pomp and circumstance of the port – now sadly lost.

Lime Street Station   The present station is not the earliest. The first was built in 1836, designed by John Cunningham with an entrance screen by Foster the Younger. This was replaced in

1846–51 with a train shed by Richard Turner and Joseph Locke assisted by Sir William Fairbairn and buildings by Sir William Tite. The train shed, 135 feet across, was the first iron roof to cover a terminus in a single span. The girders were made in Turner's Dublin works. (Turner was a contractor for the Palm House at Kew Gardens at the same time.) Rebuilding took place again in 1867 when William Baker built the iron train shed which now covers the northern half of the station. When completed it had a span of 219 feet, the largest in the world until one was built at St Pancras of 240 feet. A further extension was made in 1874–9 when an almost identical train shed (spanning 186 feet) was built over the southern half of the station. The train sheds are not as impressive as those at London termini such as St Pancras and Kings Cross because they are much lower. However, the departure from under the train sheds into the steep-sided cutting and through the rock glistening black, red, yellow and green has its own particular atmosphere. Tite's buildings survive in the yellow-golden sandstone back wall of the station across the concourse from the ticket barriers and containing ticket offices, barber's shop, various stalls etc. Major reconstruction and redevelopment is in progress at Lime Street Station (1985): part of the old wall has been replaced by plate glass decorated with engravings; hanging baskets are already up; a fresh and airy atmosphere is being created.

Alfred Waterhouse designed the LNWR's railway hotel which still stands outside the station – once adjoining the northern train shed at its western end. The flamboyant block is now offices and has recently been cleaned. It was built in 1868–71 and consists of five storeys with rows of dormers on top, chimneys and eruptions of towers and spires. The hotel had lavish plumbing for its time with 37 water closets and 8 baths serving the 200 rooms.

EUSTON
TO
MANCHESTER

Introduction

Passengers travelling to Manchester follow the original London and Birmingham Railway as far as Rugby. They then continue on the Trent Valley Railway which bypasses Birmingham. Those travelling via Stoke on Trent leave the Trent Valley Railway after Rugeley and continue northwards to Macclesfield on the North Staffordshire Railway. From Macclesfield to Manchester they follow the Manchester and Birmingham Railway. Passengers travelling via Crewe use the original Grand Junction Railway between Stafford and Crewe and then join the Manchester and Birmingham Railway to reach Manchester via Wilmslow.

The Trent Valley Railway Company was founded in 1843 with Edward Watkins as Secretary. Its aim to expand the industries already established in the Trent Valley. The first sod was cut in November 1845 by Sir Robert Peel, Prime Minister and MP for Tamworth (1830–50). He praised the self-sacrifice of the landowners: 'I assure them that there are many persons in this neighbourhood who have not scrupled to sacrifice private feeling and comfort, by consenting to their land being appropriated to the Trent Valley Railway. They have given consent from a conviction that this undertaking was one conducive to the public benefit, and that considerations of private interest should not obstruct the great one of the public good.' Nevertheless the owner of Shugborough Park was able to demand ornate entrances to the tunnel which the railway company dug under his estate.

The engineers for the line were Robert Stephenson and George Bidder and the contractor was Thomas Brassey. The line was opened in December 1847. The stations were designed by John William Livock, but many have been demolished. Tamworth and Lichfield have gone, also Stafford. The imaginative Jacobean style building at Stafford was replaced by a 1960s functional design.

The North Staffordshire Railway was centred on Stoke on Trent and it was of vital importance to the Potteries. The completion of the Trent and Mersey Canal in 1777 had made a dramatic difference to the wealth and prosperity of the area but the railway was to provide much faster, more efficient and cheaper transport. H. A. Hunt designed the stations for the North Staffordshire Railway. His favourite style was Jacobean and his masterpiece was the group of buildings at Stoke on Trent.

The Grand Junction Railway was opened on 4 July 1837 from Lime Street Station in Liverpool to a temporary terminus at Birmingham (Vauxhall). A scheme to link Birmingham with Birkenhead (the Mersey ferry-head to Liverpool) was discussed in Parliament as early as 1824 but opposed by landowners and canal owners in Cheshire, the latter fearing – quite rightly – they would lose money. One canal agent from Nantwich was overheard by George Stephenson warning local farmers that the locomotive gave off breath as poisonous as a dragon's.

Joseph Locke surveyed the line which joined George Stephenson's Liverpool and Manchester Railway at Earlestown and from there had access to Liverpool or Manchester. It was not too expensive to build – £18,846 a mile as compared with Robert Stephenson's London and Birmingham Railway's £53,000. The opening was celebrated at Stafford by the Mayor firing a 21-gun salute with ancient cannon at the approach of 'Wildfire' pulling eight 1st class coaches – the first train to Birmingham.

With the threat of competition the Liverpool and Manchester Railway and the Grand Junction amalgamated to become the London and North

Western Railway in 1846. Their headquarters were established at Crewe which was turned from a village into a thriving railway town in only a few years (see p. 88). Francis Webb, locomotive superintendant of the LNWR for 32 years, was largely responsible for building up Crewe. John Ramsbottom, famous for making the celebrated 'Lady of the Lake' class 2–2–2 express locomotive was also working at Crewe.

Though the combination of the Liverpool and Manchester Railway and the Grand Junction Railway provided Manchester with access to London, merchants and businessmen of the city wanted their own independent, direct line to the south and the Manchester and Birmingham Railway was incorporated in 1837. The first part of the line reached Stockport in 1840 and on 21 December the laying of the last stone of the 600 yard long viaduct over the Mersey was celebrated. The Manchester and Birmingham Railway built two lines (the alternative routes used by BR), the first to join the Grand Junction Railway at Crewe, the second to join up with the North Staffordshire Railway at Macclesfield. Crewe was reached in 1842. The line was first opened only as far as Sandbach (May 1842) as the Grand Junction Railway refused to allow Manchester and Birmingham trains to run on their tracks. After three months of talks, the line was finally opened all the way through to Crewe. The second line reached Macclesfield on 24 November 1845. A short tunnel into the town brought the line to the end of the North Staffordshire Railway on 18 June 1849.

EUSTON
TO
MANCHESTER

VIA
STOKE ON TRENT

Euston to Watford (see pages 20-33)
Watford to Milton Keynes (see pages 34-44)
Milton Keynes to Rugby (see pages 45-53)
Rugby to Atherstone (see pages 69-74)
Atherstone to Rugeley (see pages 75-81)

MAP 9

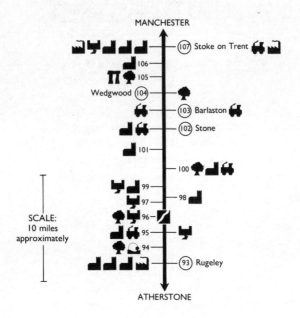

MANCHESTER

(107) Stoke on Trent

106

105

Wedgwood (104)

(103) Barlaston

(102) Stone

101

100

99

98

97

96

95

94

(93) Rugeley

SCALE:
10 miles
approximately

ATHERSTONE

94 CANNOCK CHASE is practically all that re- *L:r* mains of the great forest which once covered Staffordshire. The heath and woodland grows on the dry sandy soils of the Bunter Sandstone which crosses the Midland plain. The area has remained uncultivated because of its impractical nature and is now preserved as a place of recreation.

95 COLWICH The attractive limestone **station-** *L:r* **house** of Colwich survives beside the line. It is one of the few remaining stations designed by Livock in 1847 for the Trent Valley Railway (see p. 104) and has his distinctive gables and diamond tiles.

St Michael's Church, Colwich has a high west *L:r* tower built in 1640. Inside the church are monuments to the Anson, Sparrow and Wolesley families. Lord George Anson was a celebrated admiral and circumnavigator and his fortune – made capturing Spanish treasure galleons – was used by his brother Thomas to improve Shugborough House and Park (see p. 110). Sir William Wolesley drowned in his carriage when the mill dam suddenly burst in a thunderstorm in 1728. The four horses were also drowned but the coachman was carried to an orchard and hung on to an apple tree until the waters fell.

St Mary's Abbey was built c.1825 as Mount *R:l* Pavilion by Viscount Tamworth, son of the 7th Earl Ferrers. It is in the Tudor Gothic style with a castellated front. A Benedictine order of contemplative nuns moved into the mansion in 1834.

The line divides immediately after Colwich: to the west is the line to Stafford, Crewe and Liverpool, to the north the line to Macclesfield, Stockport and Manchester.

96 SHUGBOROUGH PARK The **Trent and** *L:r* **Mersey Canal** and the **River Trent** (which follow the railway line all the way to Stoke on Trent) flow between the railway line and Shugborough Park but it is just possible to see the house and several of the unusual buildings in the park. Shugborough House, now owned by the National Trust and open to the public, was built in 1693 for William Anson and enlarged in the 18th century by his grandson Thomas who also filled the park with the buildings designed by James 'Athenian' Stuart. Thomas Anson was a founder member of the Society of Dilettanti which sent Stuart to Athens to draw the principal buildings. These provided the inspiration for the Arch of Hadrian, the Tower of the Winds, the Doric Temple and the Lantern of Demosthenes. The 2nd Lord Lichfield inherited the property in 1854. The present Lord Lichfield occupies a flat in the house.

Shugborough House

97 INGESTRE HALL with its distinctive green *L:r* cupola is about a mile from the line and set in a park landscaped by Capability Brown in 1756. Sir Walter Chetwynd built the house early in the 17th century. The Talbots took over the estate in 1767, becoming the Earls Talbot in 1784 and the Earls of Shrewsbury in 1856. After a fire in 1882, John Birch reconstructed Jacobean-style rooms behind the original front. He also 're-Jacobeanised' parts of the house which had been altered by Nash for the 2nd Earl Talbot in 1808–10 when the Georgian style was fashionable. The Shrewsburys sold the hall in 1960. It is now used by West Bromwich Borough Council for residential courses in the arts.

98 HIXON CHURCH   St Peter's was designed *R:l* by George Gilbert Scott and consecrated in 1848. It has a north tower with a broach spire.

99 WESTON   St Andrew's Church has an early *L:r* English tower but the rest is Victorian and was designed by George Gilbert Scott and William Butterfield. **Abbeylands**, the Jacobean-style house close to the church, was also designed by Scott in 1858. They can be seen just as the train passes under the A51. **Weston Hall** is the Jacobean stone *L:r* house to the west of the church.

00 SANDON PARK   The neo-Jacobean **entrance** *R:l* **lodge** to Sandon is close to the railway line at the south end of the park. The house is not visible. It was designed by William Burn in 1852 for the 2nd Earl of Harrowby, Dudley Rider. The 2nd Earl was a politician, a fellow of the Royal Society and a promoter of reform in the treatment of tenants. He also established Staffordshire's county agricultural society. **All Saints Church** can be seen in the *R:l* park. It dates from the 13th to 14th centuries and has a Perpendicular tower.

   Sandon had its own station, opened in 1849, and the attractive red-brick **station building** is *R:l* still beside the line at the north end of the park (now a private house). A special porte-cochère was built for the Earl's carriage. **Sandon village** R:l contains several buildings designed by Sir E. Guy Dawber in c.1905 for the Sandon Estate including the Dog and Doublet Inn and the Village Club. They are in the same neo-Jacobean style as the entrance lodge.

101 **ASTON BY STONE** The church of **St** L:r **Saviour** was built in 1846 to the design of James Trubshaw. The steeple was added in 1876 and is by J. R. Botham. Aston is an attractive village, separated from the railway line by the **Trent and Mersey Canal** and the **River Trent**, both of which follow the line to Stoke.

102 **STONE** (BR)   Stone had an Augustinian Priory in the Middle Ages. The church of **St Michael** L:r (tower with pinnacles) was built in 1753–8 in the Gothic revival style. Peter de Wint, the 19th-century watercolourist, was born at Stone; also Richard Barnfield, the 16th-century poet of the Staffordshire countryside.

   Stone Station is particularly attractive. The L:r patterned brick building with stone dressings and three Dutch gables was designed by H. A. Hunt for the North Staffordshire Railway (see p. 105) and built in 1848. There are also two pretty **cottages** L:r beside the level crossings to the south and north of the station, both in the Jacobean style.

103 **BARLASTON** (BR)   After the elegant parklands of Shugborough, Ingestre and Sandon, the train now enters the industrial region of the Potteries. Barlaston was created as a model village by the architect Keith Murray. The Wedgwoods decided

to move south of Etruria in 1936 (see p. 117) to
establish a new factory and village in a park setting.
This has since spread to cover the area around the
railway line between Barlaston and Wedgwood
Stations.

Barlaston Station has fine **red-brick build-** *R&L*
ings on both sides of the line in H. A. Hunt's
favourite Jacobean style.

04 WEDGWOOD (BR)   Wedgwood Station serves
the factory established to the east of the line by the
Wedgwoods in 1936. The Wedgwoods – Josiah in
particular – were responsible for the dramatic
increase in industrial output and prosperity which
overtook the Trent Valley and neighbouring towns
at the end of the 18th century (see p. 117). South
of the station and to the east of the line is the **park** *R:l*
containing Wedgwood Hall and the village church;
north of the station and to the east is the
Wedgwood Visitor Centre which consists of
the pottery and museum where one can see all
stages of pottery creation; and paintings, exhibitions and films.

05 TRENTHAM PARK   The estate of Trentham *L:r*
covers the hillside to the west of the line. The
monument to the 1st Duke of Sutherland is
visible in the trees. It was erected in 1836 and
consists of a large bronze statue of the Duke by
Chantrey on top of a plain column which overlooks
an enormous lake designed by Capability Brown.
Trentham Park was designed by Charles Barry and
built in 1833–42 for the 2nd Duke, George
Granville Leveson-Gower. Trentham and Stafford
House in London became important social centres
in the 19th century. The Duchess was Mistress of

the Queen's Robes and kept Victoria company after the death of Prince Albert. Not only royalty but the celebrated Italian hero Garibaldi were visitors to Trentham. Disraeli renamed it Brentham in his novel *Lothair*. The house was on the grand scale but unfortunately it was demolished in 1910–12. The grounds, Trentham Gardens, are open to the public.

106 BOOTHERN CHURCH   The Victorian church of **All Saints** is on the hillside, its blackened spire *L:r* evidence of the industrial pollution which once characterised this area, the product of the coal mines of the Staffordshire coalfield and the coke ovens of the potteries.

107 STOKE ON TRENT (BR)   The embattled **church tower** south of the station with four *L:r* pinnacles belongs to **St Peter ad Vincula**. The church was built in 1826–9 and is a Commissioner's type of church, designed by Trubshaw and Johnson and built to cope with the rapidly expanding population of Stoke. Inside are monuments to the great pottery families, Josiah Wedgwood, Josiah Spode and John Bourne. Josiah Wedgwood's monument by Flaxman has the inscription, he 'converted a rude and inconsiderable manufactory into an elegant art and an important part of national commerce'.

  Stoke on Trent Station, together with the *R:l* North Stafford Hotel and housing for railway employees, were all built around Winton Square in 1847–50 to form one of the most impressive examples of railway architecture in the country. Stoke was originally at the centre of the North

Staffordshire Railway and H. A. Hunt used his
Jacobean style for the buildings which are in dark
red brick with black brick diapers and stone
dressings. The hotel is a replica of an early Jacobean
manor house. The station has a facade with three
gables and a central bay with a huge oriel window
lighting up the company's boardroom. In 1893 the
station was reconstructed behind Hunt's facade and
given an overall roof in the ridge and furrow style
supported on close spaced steel girders.

Stoke is one of the Potteries, the five towns
which became the centre of the pottery industry at
the end of the 18th century: Tunstall, Burslem,
Hanley, Stoke and Longton. Arnold Bennett, novelist of the Five Towns, renamed them Turnhill,
Bursley, Hanbridge, Knype and Longshaw. In 1925
the city of Stoke was formed as a conurbation
made up of the Potteries. The distinctive **kilns** can *L&R*
still be seen amongst the buildings close to the
railway line – bottle-shaped or conical or like
chimneys with swollen bases. They are fast dis-
appearing, however, along with many of the
factories, their work and their markets. In 1971 the
city of Stoke had more derelict land than any other
county borough in England. The prosperity which
came with the Industrial Revolution was achieved
at appalling cost, particularly in its use of child
labour. A report on the Staffordshire potteries in
1843 described the use of the children: 'with
perspiration standing on their foreheads, after
labouring like little slaves, with the mercury 20
degrees below freezing ... many die of consump-
tion, asthma and acute inflammation.' The magnifi-
cence of Stoke on Trent's **Town Hall** reflects only *L:r*
one side of life in the Potteries. It was designed by
Henry Ward and built in 1834–50. The centre has a

MAP 10

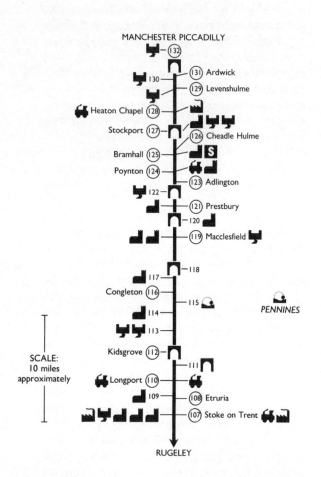

MANCHESTER PICCADILLY
132
131 Ardwick
130
129 Levenshulme
Heaton Chapel 128
Stockport 127
126 Cheadle Hulme
Bramhall 125 **S**
Poynton 124
123 Adlington
122
121 Prestbury
120
119 Macclesfield
118
117
Congleton 116
115
PENNINES
114
113
Kidsgrove 112
111
Longport 110
109
108 Etruria
107 Stoke on Trent

SCALE:
10 miles
approximately

RUGELEY

Stoke on Trent Potteries

giant upper portico of unfluted Ionic columns and can be seen from the train.

Our Lady of the Angels is the large yellow *L:r* and red brick Gothic style building north of the station. The Roman Catholic convent was designed by Charles Hansom in 1857 and enlarged by A. E. Purdie in 1884–5.

Holy Trinity, Hartshill Road is on the hillside *L:r* above the railway line and just beyond Stoke Infirmary. It was designed by George Gilbert Scott in 1842. It was paid for by Herbert Minton and is lavishly adorned inside with Minton tiles.

108 ETRURIA (BR) Etruria was the centre of the Wedgwood empire. Josiah Wedgwood (1730–95) came from a family of potters in Burslem and after rising to become a master-potter in 1759 and Queen's potter in 1762, he bought a site between Burslem and Stoke in 1766 for £300, called it Etruria and built a factory, village and mansion. The warehouses and kilns along the canal were demolished in the 1960s but the canal itself is a result of Wedgwood's energy. He was ardent in his campaign to have the canal built: it would make a dramatic difference to his own problems of transport. The Trent and Mersey Canal was finally opened in 1777 (see p. 80). Etruria is the site for the 1986 National Garden Festival and will remain as a featured garden after the Festival.

109 WOLSTANTON CHURCH   The spire of the high Victorian **St Margaret's** can just be seen to the west.   *L:r*

110 LONGPORT (BR)   The station has the familiar pretty North Staffordshire buildings: **red brick and Jacobean style** to the west, single storey **red brick with limestone trims** to the windows *L:r* to the east.   *R:l*

There is considerable industry along this part of the Trent Valley with steel works and collieries and the living and dead pottery works jostling for space close to the canal and railway. Beyond Westport Lake is the pottery town of **Tunstall**. George *R:l* Moore described the landscape of the Potteries in *A Mummer's Wife*: 'It was one of those terrible cauldrons in which man melts and moulds this huge age of iron ... wide widths of walls, bald rotundities of pottery ovens, reigned supreme; before them nature had disappeared, and the shrill scream of the steam train as it rolled solemnly up the incline seemed man's cry of triumph over vanquished nature.'

111 HARECASTLE TUNNELS   The mile-long *R:l* railway tunnel which was dug in 1848 is now by-passed. Parallel to the railway tunnel but considerably older are the **Harecastle Canal**

Tunnels for the Trent and Mersey Canal. The first tunnel was dug in 1766–77 by James Brindley and is 2,880 yards long. The second, by Telford, is 2,926 yards long and was dug in 1824–7. Brindley (1716–72), under the patronage of the Duke of Bridgewater (see p. 128), was responsible for designing and building 360 miles of canals in the North of England and Midlands.

112 KIDSGROVE (BR) The train passes through a short tunnel to reach Kidsgrove Station.

113 RAMSDELL HALL The impressive baronial *L:r* gates just across the canal are the entrance to Ramsdell Hall, a fine red brick mansion built c.1720–60. Slightly further north is the **Old** *L:r* **Parsonage**, a handsome white house with Corinthian columns supporting the porch.

114 ASTBURY CHURCH The Decorated tower *L:r* and recessed spire of Astbury church can be seen about a mile from the line. Astbury has another tower at the western end, a three-storeyed porch added in the late 15th century, making the church one of the 'most exciting' in Cheshire (N. Pevsner). The countryside here is rich pastureland, a contrast to the industrial valley to the south.

115 The hills to the east are the western edge of the **Pennines**. The moorlands of the Pennines are *L:r* formed of Millstone and Moorstone Grit and, at this point, Yoredale Rock. There are two outcrops of the dark Yoredale Rock above the railway line: the **Old Man of Mow**, 1,100 feet high, opposite *R:l* Ramsdell Hall, and **The Cloud**, 1125 feet high, just past Congleton. The Old Man of Mow or Mow Cop once had flourishing gritstone quarries.

116 **CONGLETON** (BR)   The North Staffordshire Railway Company's familiar Tudor-Jacobean-style building at Congleton has been replaced by a new red-brick station. Congleton became an important centre for silk-weaving in the 18th century. John Clayton of Stockport and Nathaniel Pattison of London established Clayton's Mill in c.1752. By 1817 the town had 17 silk mills and 5 cotton mills.

117 **BUGLAWTON CHURCH St John the** L:r **Evangelist** was designed in 1840 by R. B. Rampling and has a recessed spire.

118 **THE CONGLETON AND DANE VIADUCTS** carry the railway line over the Biddulph branch of the North Staffordshire Railway, the **Trent and Mersey Canal** and the **River Dane**, and offer fine views of the countryside to the west and east with the rocky outcrop 'The Cloud' rising above the **Dane Valley**. The viaducts were designed by J. C. Forsyth, engineer for the North Staffordshire Railway, and were completed in 1849. The Congleton, to the south, has 16 arches 130 feet high; the Dane is built of blue brick and has 20 arches. They mark the boundary between **Staffordshire** and **Cheshire**.

119 **MACCLESFIELD** (BR)   The steeple of **St Paul's** church dominates the town from its L:r elevated position just south of the station. It is a Commissioners' church and was designed by W. Hayley and built in 1843–4.

    The parish church of **St Michael** (founded by L:r

Queen Eleanor at the end of the 13th century) is on top of the steep escarpment just north of the station. The tower is Perpendicular but most of the church was rebuilt in 1898–1901 by Sir Arthur Blomfield. The unusual Pardon Brass is inside. It is to Roger Legh who died in 1506 and gives him the confident assurance that the pardon for offering 5 Paternosters, 5 Aves and one Creed is 26,000 years and 26 days.

Macclesfield was built up on the manufacture of silk and cotton. The first silk mill was established in 1743 by Charles Roe who also started copper works 15 years later. By 1900 there were 30 silk mills in the town and many cotton factories.

Messrs Arighi, Bianchi

Messrs Arighi, Bianchi survives from the late R:l
19th century, a fine example and immaculately
maintained, with a front of arched cast iron and
glass.

120 **HURDSFIELD CHURCH Holy Trinity** is R:l
another Commissioners' church, built with the
intention of christianising the expanding workforce. It was designed by William Hayley and built
in 1837–9. Its limestone tower (recently cleaned)
overlooks the industrial estate of Hurdsfield in
which a diversity of industries are being developed
including the making of pharmaceutical products.

The **tunnel** through which the train passes below
Hurdsfield was dug in 1849.

121 **PRESTBURY** (BR)   With a local railway service
(the line between Cheadle and Macclesfield was
opened in 1845) and the close proximity of
Macclesfield and Stockport, Prestbury has been
developed as a commuter village for the most
prosperous workers of the area. **St Peter's** has a L:r
medieval tower but was rebuilt in the late 19th
century. It is in one of the prettiest and most
visited villages in Cheshire, rich in timbered
cottages and well-tended gardens.

122 **MILL HOUSE, ADLINGTON**   After a short L:r
tunnel the train passes the fine timber-framed
E-shaped Mill House Farm which is close to the
line. It was built in 1603 by the Legh family as a
Dower House. The Leghs inherited the Adlington
estates in 1315. Colonel Thomas Legh was an
active Royalist during the Civil Wars and his widow
Ann lived in the Dower House for many years. The

house has stone slated roofs and stone stacks, wood mullioned windows and casements with leaded lights.

23 **ADLINGTON** (BR)   The trustees of the Adlington estates (the landowner Charles Richard Bonastre Legh was a minor) were paid £12,712 3s 9d by the LNWR as purchase money for land taken by the railway and in compensation for damage caused. Just over 56 acres of Legh land were used through Adlington, Butley and Prestbury.

24 **POYNTON** (BR)   The first station was some distance from the village to the south and closed when the present one was opened on 1 August 1887. This consists of a smart **red-brick house** *R:l* with ornate brackets painted mustard yellow. **St** *R:l* **George's** is a Victorian church, its steeple designed by J. Medland and Henry Taylor.

Just north of Poynton the train crosses the boundary between **Cheshire** and **Greater Manchester**.

25 **BRAMHALL** (BR)   Bramhall has been intensively developed since the 1930s with housing estates surrounding the **golf course** and the grounds of *R:l* Bramhall Hall (which is one of the finest timber-framed houses in the country and open to the public). **St Michael's** is an Edwardian church; the *R:l* brick tower, by G. G. Pace, was added in 1960–3.

26 **CHEADLE HULME** (BR)   The first station at Cheadle Hulme was opened in 1842, a quarter of a mile away on the Manchester to Crewe line. The present station was opened in 1866 at the junction

with the line to Macclesfield (though the buildings are 20th-century). The railway line has moved away from the ridge of hills to the east and the view to the north is of the enormous industrial conurbation which surrounds Manchester – chimneys and spires, patches of wasteland, occasional trees, old and new factories and housing estates.

127 **STOCKPORT** (BR)   The most spectacular feature of Stockport is the railway **viaduct** which carries the line high over the **River Mersey**.

Stockport Station has red-brick platform buildings patterned with black brick and yellow brick window trims. The awnings and valancing are painted a sandy colour and supported by elegant brackets. The signal boxes at either end of the station are in the same red and black brick with sandy coloured wooden tops.

Like Macclesfield (see p. 120) **Stockport** began to expand with the silk industry followed by the cotton industry. One of the first cotton mills was built by Sir George Warren on the site of the medieval castle. It was specially designed as a circular building with battlements. The old town was close to the River Mersey in the valley rising steeply up to the market place and parish church. **St Mary's** was mostly rebuilt in 1813–17 to the R:l design of Lewis Wyatt and is in a Perpendicular Gothic style with a west tower. John Wainwright, composer of the tune to the well-known hymn 'Christians Awake', was organist of St Mary's and was buried in the church in 1768. The **Market** R:l **Hall** has an iron and glass cover erected in 1861. Throughout the 19th century houses and factories began to spread over the higher ground on both sides of the river. Hat-making became an important local industry, followed by engineering. From the viaduct there is a good view of the mills, warehouses and factories below and also of **Merseyway**, a pedestrian way made by covering up part of the river and now part of the new shopping precinct. George Watson Buck designed the viaduct which is 600 yards long, has 27 arches and is 111 feet above the bed of the Mersey. It was built for the Manchester and Birmingham Railway and before it was completed (1840) there was a temporary station at the north end – where the LNWR goods warehouse is now sited – which lasted until 1959 as Heaton Norris.

The Wren-style tower of the **Town Hall** is *R:l* visible to the east of the station. The Town Hall was designed by Sir Alfred Brumwell Thomas and built in 1904–8 of white stone.

28 HEATON CHAPEL (BR) The station was opened in January 1852. The red-brick **ticket** *L:r* **office** above the cutting is patterned with black brick. The Edwardian factory of **McVities & Price** *R:l* **Biscuits** is beside the line.

29 LEVENSHULME (BR) The station was opened in August 1842. The half-timbered two-storey house just by the line is **Slade Hall**. It was built in *L:r* 1585 and the timbering is mostly in a herring-bone pattern. The back of the house is of early 19th-century brick. Inside, there is a frieze in one of the rooms of naive plasterwork depicting hunting scenes.

30 MANCHESTER UNIVERSITY The **high** *L:r* **tower** with a steep pyramid roof belongs to the east range of Manchester University and was built in 1883–7. The university began as Owens College (1851) and moved to its present site in 1873. Alfred Waterhouse began work as architect of the new buildings in 1870. The University, together with the Institution of Science and Technology, the Municipal College of Technology and the College of Art, have recently been brought together on a vast campus more familiar in American universities, under the plan of Sir Hugh Wilson and Lewis Wormesley.

Manchester University

131 ARDWICK STATION (BR) is on the line to *R:l*
Huddersfield and Leeds. In 1830, just before the
railway was built, Ardwick was 'a fashionable
residential quarter for Manchester merchants'.

132 MANCHESTER (BR) Manchester Piccadilly
Station is approached on a **viaduct** of 16 arches
from which the flamboyant clock tower of the old
Magistrates' Court in Minshull Street can be *L:r*
seen. This Italian Gothic-style building adorned
with gables and turrets was built in 1871 and
designed by Thomas Worthington.

    Manchester Piccadilly was opened as London
Road in 1862 and enlarged in 1881 when the iron-
and glass-roofed train sheds were erected. The
train sheds are supported by iron pillars painted
white and blue and decorated with leafy capitals
and ornate brackets. The front of London Road was
'a beautiful stone building in the Italian style': now it
is dull glass and steel. The station was rebuilt in
1960 as part of the plan to adopt the 25kV system
of electric traction and was renamed Piccadilly on
the opening on 12 September. R. L. Moorcroft,
Midland Region's architect, was the designer.

    A visitor to Manchester in 1851 wrote to warn
fellow travellers: 'dreadful fires occur occasionally
in Manchester. If such a catastrophe should take
place during the stay of a visitor, he should
immediately pull on an overcoat, even though it be
midnight, and join in the crowd. An excellent police
of 300 officers and men renders the streets quite
safe at all hours; and a fire of an old cotton factory,
where the floors are saturated with oil and grease,
is indeed a fearfully imposing sight. It also affords an
opportunity of some familiar conversation with the
factory hands.' Even in 1926 there were plenty of

factories to catch fire, as a continental visitor observed: 'At Manchester since the war 400 large new factories for cotton spinning have been built, several of them of the size of the Royal Palace in Berlin, and thousands of smoking obelisks of the steam engines 80 to 180 feet high destroy all impression of church steeples.'

The prosperity of Manchester was made out of cotton and cheap factory labour. Weaving flourished in the Middle Ages after Edward III settled a colony of Flemish weavers in the town but it was not until the 18th century that expansion began. The River Irwell was made navigable in 1721. Then the Duke of Bridgewater employed James Brindley to cut a canal from his coal mine at Worsley to Manchester. This was extended to Runcorn in 1776 and the means was created by which raw cotton could be transported direct to the centre of Manchester. St Peter's Square, the site of Alfred Waterhouse's extraordinary gothic Town Hall and Charles Barry's Grecian Royal Institution, is also a grim reminder of St Peter's Fields where the Peterloo Massacre took place in 1819. Many of the rich merchants of Manchester who paid for the city's monumental public buildings forced their workers to endure appalling conditions in their factories. Friedrich Engels's *Condition of the Working Class in England* (1844) gives a moving account of the deprivation experienced by Manchester workers while their employers grew rich. De Tocqueville remarked on the 'pure gold' made in Manchester flowing from the 'filthy sewer'; the novelist Mrs Gaskell revealed the inequalities in *Mary Barton, A Tale of Manchester Life* (1848).

EUSTON
TO
MANCHESTER

VIA
CREWE

MAP 11

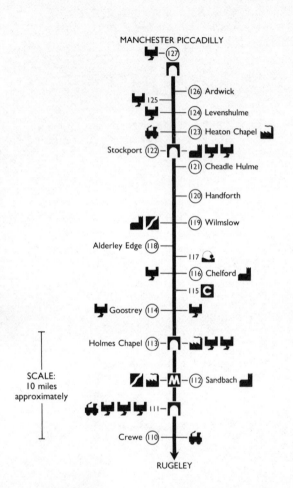

MANCHESTER PICCADILLY

(127)

(126) Ardwick

125

(124) Levenshulme

(123) Heaton Chapel

Stockport (122)

(121) Cheadle Hulme

(120) Handforth

(119) Wilmslow

Alderley Edge (118)

117

(116) Chelford

115

Goostrey (114)

Holmes Chapel (113)

(112) Sandbach

111

Crewe (110)

RUGELEY

SCALE:
10 miles
approximately

110 CREWE When the Grand Junction railway arrived at Crewe in 1837 the population of about 200 lived in small farms and cottages. By 1842, the station was the focus of four railway lines and the locomotive works which had been moved from Edge Hill was about to begin production. The railway company built houses, churches and schools, and by 1851 the population had risen to 4,571. The salaries of the curate and the schoolmaster were paid by the company which also provided a doctor and two policemen, organised the supply of mains water, the emptying of ash pits, cess pools and privies and even set up a savings bank for its employees. Four classes of house were built: 'first, the villa-style lodges of the superior officer; next a kind of ornamental Gothic constitutes the house of the next in authority; the engineers domiciled in detached mansions, which accommodate four families, with gardens and separate entrances; and last the labourer delights in neat cottages of four apartments, the entrances within ancient porches'.

Crewe Station consists of three broad island platforms each with creamy yellow brick buildings decorated with red and dark blue brick dressings, all under a lateral train shed. The bay windows have Greek heads on the keystones. Immediately next to the station is the **Crewe Arms** built in the *R:1* Jacobean style and opened in 1837. It was taken over by the LNWR as their railway hotel in 1864. Rather less decorative is the 13-storey block by the station which is **Rail House**, designed by F. S. Curtis and R. C. Moorcroft, British Rail architects, and erected in 1967–8.

North of Crewe Station (at North Crewe Junction) the **line divides**: the old Grand Junction

Railway continues northwards to Liverpool; the old Manchester and Birmingham Railway takes passengers north-east towards Manchester.

111 THE CHESHIRE COUNTRYSIDE Once the suburbs of Crewe have been left behind, the train enters the rolling countryside of the Central Cheshire Plain. Cheshire is one of the least known of English counties, but the countryside is not unattractive. Dotted with small lakes or meres, it is typically English: lush, gentle, pastoral, with prosperous farms, large estates and many half-timbered cottages.

About three miles to the north-east of Crewe the line passes close by **Railway Farm**, two *L:r* storeys, red brick with a barn beside it; then **Brook Farm** and, further away among the trees, *L:r* **Elton Hall**. This is just before the **Elton Embankment** – a cellular embankment built with adjustable rugby-style goal posts to prevent the overhead wires (the line was electrified in 1960) from sagging in an area where subsidence occurs (Rex Christiansen, *The West Midlands*, Newton Abbot, 1973).

112 SANDBACH (BR) Sandbach is about two miles to the east. The town is famous for its two Saxon crosses in the cobbled marketplace. The crosses are believed to have been erected to commemorate the conversion of Penda King of Mercia and his marriage to a Christian princess. Sandbach is one of the Cheshire salt towns: it is also the home of the Fodens Motor Works, famous for their prize-winning brass band.

Sandbach Station is really in the village of

Elworth. **St Peter's** is the parish church, rock- R:l
faced with a bellcote, designed by John Matthews.
It is a Commissioner's church, erected in 1845–6
with the intention of bringing religion to the
population which was rapidly expanding with the
development of local industries (notice the red-
brick **Elworth Wire Mills**). R:l

Just north of the station the line to Middlewich
branches to the north-west. Middlewich is the
second oldest salt town in Cheshire, connected to
Elworth and Sandbach by not only the railway but
the A533 and the **Trent and Mersey Canal**. L:r
Industry is intensive along these lines of communication (chemicals works and beyond, a salt
factory).

The railway line crosses the **M6** halfway between
Sandbach and Holmes Chapel.

113 **HOLMES CHAPEL** (BR) **Fisons** is just south R:l
of the station. The impressive building is one of
their pharmaceutical production sites. To the north
of the station the train passes over the **Dane
Viaduct**, designed by G. W. Buck and built for the
Manchester and Birmingham Railway in 1840–1. It
has 23 arches 63 feet wide and is 105 feet high.
There are good views from the viaduct of the
Cheshire countryside. **Saltersford Hall** (half- R:l
timbered) is on the hillside and then **Saltersford** R:l
Farm down in the valley, their names reflecting
the most important local industry.

114 **GOOSTREY** (BR) is to the east of the station.
Just to the north is **Blackden Manor** and on the R:l
other side of the line, as the train crosses a long
embankment, **Blackden Hall**. The Hall is close to L:r

the line, a very attractive timber-framed house.

115 JODRELL BANK Although the train passes Jodrell Bank in a cutting a mile long, there is a clear view of the **observatory**. Sir Bernard Lovell was *R:l* the first director of the radio astronomy laboratory of Manchester University (now the Nuffield Radio Astronomy Laboratories). The first instrument – Mark I – was erected in 1952–7 and was able, just before completion, to track the first Sputnik. The circular bowl of Mark I is 250 feet in diameter; the telescope is one of the largest fully steerable radio telescopes in the world.

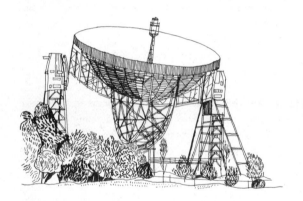

Observatory, Jodrell Bank

116 CHELFORD (BR)   The new houses close to the line are on an estate called **Mere Court**. The **old** *L:r* **village** is a mile to the south east. Its Georgian **parish church** has a Victorian spire.   *R:l*

117 ALDERLEY EDGE   The ridge thickly covered *R:l* with trees which can be seen to the east of the line is Alderley Edge. 650 feet high and 2 miles long, the

ridge provides a fine viewing-point for the surrounding countryside of Cheshire and Lancashire. It
is associated with many local myths and legends and
features in the writings of Alan Garner. One spot
on the ridge is supposed to be where a countryman
was led by a wizard and shown the iron gates of a
cave in which warriors were sleeping. A stone on
top of Alderley Edge marks where a beacon flared
to warn of the approach of the Spanish Armada to
the shores of England.

118 **ALDERLEY EDGE** (BR) When the railway
arrived at Alderley Edge in 1842 the village was
transformed into a commuter town for affluent
Mancunians, full of fine early Victorian houses. The
bright station, recently painted, shows that Alderley (like Wilmslow to the north) is still heavily used
by railway commuters. It offers the combination of
easy and quick access both to the centre of
Manchester and to the pastoral delights of
Cheshire. A considerably long time before the
railway came to Alderley it was a camp site for
mesolithic hunters. Their flint caves, flakes and
microliths have been found in the area.

119 **WILMSLOW** (BR) Just like Alderley Edge,
Wilmslow developed as a commuter town for
Manchester and still has a well-kept, heavily used
railway station (red-brick, cream-painted pillars,
sandy painted decorative valances). The parish
church of **St Bartholomew's** is on the banks of *L:r*
the **River Bollin** (the River Bollin meets the
River Dean at Twinnies Bridge in Wilmslow). It is
mostly 16th century, including the tower, and
inside has several fine 16th-century monuments,
and a 15th-century brass to Robert Booth and his

St Bartholomew's, Wilmslow

wife, Booth's right foot resting on a dog representing faithfulness. Some of the glass in the church is by Morris and Co.

Wilmslow was the home of Samuel Finney, portrait painter, favourite of Queen Caroline and ruthless magistrate. He was so successful in controlling drunkenness and disorder in the town in the 18th century that Wilmslow has had a reputation for respectability ever since.

120 HANDFORTH (BR)   New houses now join up Wilmslow and Handforth. Manchester's suburbs are spreading as the population within a mere 2½ miles of the city has passed 10 million.

121 CHEADLE HULME (BR)   The first station at Cheadle Hulme was opened in 1842 a quarter mile south. The present station was opened in 1866 at the junction with the line to Macclesfield (though the buildings are 20th century) and serves the lines to Manchester from Crewe and Stoke on Trent. The view to the north is of the enormous industrial conurbation which surrounds Manchester – chimneys and spires, patches of wasteland, occasional trees, old and new factories and housing estates.

22 STOCKPORT (BR)   The most spectacular feature of Stockport is the railway **viaduct** which carries the line high over the **River Mersey**.

Stockport Station has red-brick platform buildings patterned with black brick and yellow brick window trims. The awnings and valancing are painted a sandy colour and supported by elegant brackets. The signal boxes at either end of the station are in the same red and black brick with sandy-coloured wooden tops.

Like Macclesfield (see p. 120) **Stockport** began to expand with the silk industry followed by the cotton industry. One of the first cotton mills was built by Sir George Warren on the site of the medieval castle. It was specially designed as a circular building with battlements. The old town was close to the River Mersey in the valley rising steeply up to the market place and parish church. **St Mary's** was mostly rebuilt in 1813–17 to the *R:l* design of Lewis Wyatt and is in a Perpendicular Gothic style with a west tower. John Wainwright, organist of St Mary's, was buried in the church in 1768. He composed the tune of the well-known hymn 'Christians Awake'. The **Market Hall** has an *R:l* iron and glass cover erected in 1861. Throughout the 19th century houses and factories began to spread over the higher ground on both sides of the river. Hat-making became an important local industry, followed by engineering. From the viaduct there is a good view of the mills, ware-houses and factories below and also of **Mersey-way**, a pedestrian way made by covering up part of the river and now part of the new shopping precinct. George Watson Buck designed the viaduct which is 600 yards long, has 27 arches and is 111 feet above the bed of the Mersey. It was built for the Manchester and Birmingham Railway and before it was completed (1840) there was a temporary station at the north end – where the LNWR goods warehouse is now sited – which lasted until 1959 as Heaton Norris.

The Wren-style tower of the **Town Hall** is *R:l* visible to the east of the station. It was designed by Sir Alfred Brumwell Thomas and built in 1904–8 of white stone.

123 **HEATON CHAPEL** (BR) The station was opened in January 1852. The red-brick **ticket** *L:r* **office** above the cutting is patterned with black brick. The Edwardian factory of **McVities & Price** *R:l* **Biscuits** is beside the line.

124 **LEVENSHULME** (BR) The station was opened in August 1842. The half-timbered two-storey house just by the line is **Slade Hall**. It was built in *L:r* 1585 and the timbering is mostly in a herring-bone pattern. The back of the house is of early 19th-century brick. In one of the rooms inside there is a frieze of naive plasterwork depicting hunting scenes.

125 **MANCHESTER UNIVERSITY** The **high** *L:r* **tower** with a steep pyramid roof belongs to the east range of Manchester University and was built

in 1883–7. The university began as Owens College (1851) and moved to its present site in 1873. Alfred Waterhouse began work as architect of the new buildings in 1870. The University, together with the Institution of Science and Technology, the Municipal College of Technology and the College of Art, have recently been brought together on a vast campus more familiar in American universities, under the plan of Sir Hugh Wilson and Lewis Wormesley.

126 ARDWICK STATION is on the line to Huddersfield and Leeds. In 1830 just before the railway was built, Ardwick was 'a fashionable residential quarter for Manchester merchants'. R:l

127 MANCHESTER (BR) Manchester Piccadilly Station is approached on a **viaduct** of 16 arches from which the flamboyant clock tower of the old **Magistrates' Court** in Minshull Street can be seen. This Italian Gothic style building adorned with gables and turrets was built in 1871 and designed by Thomas Worthington. L:r

    Manchester Piccadilly was opened as London Road in 1862 and enlarged in 1881 when the iron- and glass-roofed train sheds were erected. The train sheds are supported by iron pillars painted white and blue and decorated with leafy capitals and ornate brackets. The front of London Road was 'a beautiful stone building in the Italian style': now it is dull glass and steel. The station was rebuilt in 1960 as part of the plan to adopt the 25kV system of electric traction and was renamed Piccadilly on the opening on 12 September. R. L. Moorcroft, Midland Region's architect, was the designer.

    A visitor to Manchester in 1851 wrote to warn

fellow travellers: 'dreadful fires occur occasionally in Manchester. If such a catastrophe should take place during the stay of a visitor, he should immediately pull on an overcoat, even though it be midnight, and join in the crowd. An excellent police of 300 officers and men renders the streets quite safe at all hours; and a fire of an old cotton factory, where the floors are saturated with oil and grease, is indeed a fearfully imposing sight. It also affords an opportunity of some familiar conversation with the factory hands.' Even in 1926 there were plenty of factories to catch fire, as a continental visitor observed: 'At Manchester since the war 400 large new factories for cotton spinning have been built, several of them of the size of the Royal Palace in Berlin, and thousands of smoking obelisks of the steam engines 80 to 180 feet high destroy all impression of church steeples.'

The prosperity of Manchester was made out of cotton and cheap factory labour. Weaving flourished in the Middle Ages after Edward III settled a colony of Flemish weavers in the town but it was not until the 18th century that expansion began. The River Irwell was made navigable in 1721. Then the Duke of Bridgewater employed James Brindley to cut a canal from his coal mine at Worsley to Manchester. This was extended to Runcorn in 1776 and the means was created by which raw cotton could be transported direct to the centre of Manchester. St Peter's Square, the site of Alfred Waterhouse's extraordinary gothic Town Hall and Charles Barry's Grecian Royal Institution, is also a grim reminder of St Peter's Fields where the Peterloo Massacre took place in 1819. Many of the rich merchants of Manchester who paid for the city's monumental public buildings forced their workers to endure appalling conditions in their factories. Friedrich Engels's *Condition of the Working Class in England* (1844) gives a moving account of the deprivation experienced by Manchester workers while their employers grew rich. De Tocquerville remarked on the 'pure gold' made in Manchester flowing from the 'filthy sewer'; the novelist Mrs Gaskell revealed the inequalities in *Mary Barton, A Tale of Manchester Life* (1848).

BRITISH
RAILWAY
JOURNEYS

Other volumes available in the series:

Paddington to the West
(Plymouth, Cardiff, Bristol)
ISBN 0 947795 50 2, 144pp., £2.95

King's Cross to the North
(Edinburgh)
ISBN 0 947795 65 0, 96pp., £2.95

Victoria and Waterloo to the South
(Brighton, Dover, Southampton)
ISBN 0 947795 75 8, 144pp., £2.95